DALE CARNEGIE

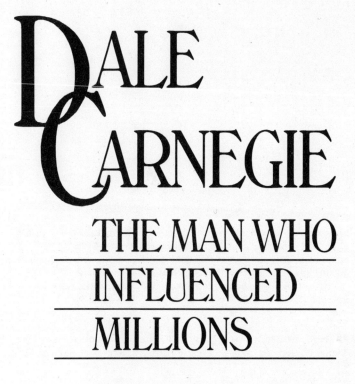

DALE CARNEGIE

THE MAN WHO
INFLUENCED
MILLIONS

GILES KEMP and
EDWARD CLAFLIN

ST. MARTIN'S PRESS
NEW YORK

All characterizations of Dale Carnegie Course participants are based on composite portraits. Names have been changed to protect anonymity.

Design by Glen M. Edelstein

Library of Congress Cataloging-in-Publication Data

Kemp, Giles.
     Dale Carnegie: the man who influenced millions / Giles Kemp and Edward Claflin.
          p.   cm.
     ISBN 0-312-02896-2
     1. Carnegie, Dale, 1888–1955.   2. Carnegie, Dale, 1888–1955—Influence.   3. Conduct of life.   4. Teachers—United States—Biography. 5. Orators—United States—Biography.   6. Authors, American—20th century—Biography. I. Claflin, Edward.   II. Title.
CT275.C3114K46   1989   973.91'092'4—dc19   [B]   89-4078

First Edition
10 9 8 7 6 5 4 3 2 1

To Walters Kemp

To Beecher Claflin

ACKNOWLEDGMENTS

The story of Dale Carnegie that you will find in these pages involves the close interweaving of a man's life with the course that led to his fame.

Since that course is still very much alive, our thanks must first go to the instructors and participants who breathe *their* lives into it and who have shared so many of their "Dale Carnegie experiences" with us.

For biographical details, we are indebted to many people who gave generously of their time to discuss various aspects of the Dale Carnegie story. At the risk of omitting a few, we would like to express our appreciation to Herb Alexander, Frank Ashby, Carol Cook Carlisle, Donna Dale Carnegie, Brenda Crom, Dennis Engel, Charlie Goldsmith, John Harrington, Mary Hedge, Bob Hower, J. Weldon Jackson, Margaret Kelley, Stew Leonard, Dennis Levy, Andrea Nierenberg, Dr. Norman Vincent Peale, Peter Schwed, Leon Shimkin, Lowell Thomas, Jr., Russ Wernex, and Fred White.

From Edward Claflin, a special note of appreciation to Holly LaMon at Brookside Press—whose comments, gibes, and proofreading skills were as crucial as her adeptness with Wordstar.

There are times in the course of any book when friends are most emphatically needed to influence people. We are especially grateful to Jane Dystel, our agent, who wholeheartedly believed in this book from its inception—and was unflagging in her campaign to see it published. Our thanks also to Tom McCormack, Toni Lopopolo, Stacia Friedman, and Maryanne Mazzola—the great team at St. Martin's Press whose enthusiasm for this book was most welcome.

The labors of book-writing invariably consume at least 300 percent more time than anyone can foretell, and we are grateful to our families who patiently bore the brunt of absences, departures, and, yes, even bad manners.

From EC: Thank you, Diana, for your sheer belief; and bless you, Jessica and Abigail, for being just regular kids.

From GK: Thank you, Barbara, for putting up with my lapsed commitment to avoid the three C's; and to Rebecca and David, thanks for reminding me of the magic of enthusiasm.

CONTENTS

TO THE READER

D ALE CARNEGIE MAY HAVE BEEN HIS OWN WORST enemy. Famed for his courses on public speaking, his own speaking style was rambling, his accent a midwestern twang. When he was the number one best-selling author in America, he gave interviews in which he expressed astonishment at his fame and insisted that he had nothing profound to say to people.

Although his courses inspired some of the foremost political leaders, broadcast journalists, and inspirational speakers of his time, he staunchly insisted that his methods were only common sense and that his teachings were for the common man.

Dale Carnegie was also a man misunderstood by many who

saw only his public image and had no direct experience with his teachings.

Although he advocated spontaneity and sincerity, many saw him as the proponent of methods that were cynical, conniving, and manipulative.

One of the great teachers of all time—whose teaching techniques have spread across the globe and whose message touched millions of lives—he was, at best, shrugged off by academics and, at the worst, heartily scorned.

A man who dedicated his life to giving hope to everyday working people, he was often derided by intellectuals as a pandering preacher of blind acceptance.

A writer who dealt frankly and openly with agnosticism, emptiness, psychosomatic illness, and suicide, he was branded a starry-eyed optimist.

Although his course had been in existence for twenty-four years when his first popular book was published, *How to Win Friends and Influence People* was the key to Dale Carnegie's fame. First published in 1936 by Simon & Schuster, it became an overnight success. It went on to sell more than 15 million copies.

To someone who has never encountered Dale Carnegie's prose before, it seems a curious book to be a best-seller. Its language, message, and examples are rooted in the vernacular of the nineteen twenties and thirties. Anyone looking at the four sections of the book will see that, yes, this is a book on how to manipulate people. These sections are "Fundamental Techniques in Handling People," "Six Ways to Make People Like You," "How to Win People to Your Way of Thinking," and "Be a Leader: How to Change People Without Giving Offense or Arousing Resentment." Chapter titles reveal the homespun nature of the Dale Carnegie philosophy, with phrases such as "If You Want to Gather Honey, Don't Kick Over the Beehive," "If You're Wrong, Admit It," and "No One Likes to Take Orders."

Are these the keys to the Dale Carnegie kingdom?

And, if so, what was all the excitement about?

More to the point, are such common-sense aphorisms still relevant today?

The answers are certainly not to be found in the writing. The text is appealing enough, the stories have a certain quaint charm, and the quotations are apt. The principles that serve as action steps are about what you would expect to find in most self-help psychology books today. But Dale Carnegie's prose certainly isn't brilliant. He repeats himself. He contradicts himself.

Nor was it the man, apart from the book, who made the sales figures soar. This was no Bill Cosby or Lee Iacocca. He was never on a par with the most popular communicators of his time, men like Lowell Thomas and Edward R. Murrow. In his radio appearances no charisma came through—because it wasn't there. He seemed like a good guy, sincere enough, a little schoolmarmish at times, though harmless and well-meaning for all that.

If it was not the book who made the man, and not the man who made the book, then what *was* going on?

We wondered.

And then we began to look at the course.

The Dale Carnegie Course in Public Speaking and Human Relations was begun in 1912 by Carnegie (his last name was then spelled Carnagey) in a YMCA night school on 125th Street in New York's Harlem. With only a few interruptions (World War I, a bout of novel writing that took him to Europe, and a venture with Lowell Thomas), Carnegie continually taught, refined, and promoted the course up until his death in 1955.

More than three million men and women have graduated from the fourteen-week, fourteen-session program. In 1988 there were over 165,000 graduates of the Dale Carnegie Course in the United States alone, and the course is conducted in more than sixty other countries around the world.

The list of esteemed graduates is long. Many of those graduates say that the course changed their lives. Among the recent notables are Lee Iacocca ("To this day, I'm a great believer in the Dale Carnegie Institute.... I've sent dozens of introverted guys to Dale Carnegie at the company's expense."); Linda Gray (of "Dallas" fame); Tom Monaghan (founder of Domino's Pizza); John

Emery (of Emery Air Freight); and Stew Leonard (who owns the largest dairy store in the world). The list of entrepreneurs, executives, politicians, and performers is extensive. Perhaps even more significant, the course, in the nineteen eighties, has experienced a surge of popularity. Many of tomorrow's speakers, politicians, sales professionals, and business leaders are taking the course today.

As students of the Dale Carnegie phenomenon, the authors became interested in the course both for what it is—which is a unique group experience—and for what it says about Dale Carnegie.

In Dale Carnegie, we finally concluded, we have the unique situation of a man who best expressed himself *through a course that was a living experience*. But the course was also an invention that the inventor could not escape. Throughout his life, there were times when Carnegie attempted to leave his invention behind and go on to other accomplishments. After each hiatus, however, Carnegie returned to the course—partly out of necessity (he could always make a living teaching "Dale Carnegie" classes) and partly because it was, simply, what he did best. So it became the repository of all the aspirations that he had in other areas—as an orator, a salesman, an actor, a novelist, a theatrical producer, and a businessman.

Dale Carnegie made the course his lifework. In it he concentrated his life experiences. The course was his laboratory with people. Because it was his own creation, he could alter the format. He worked out ways to increase positive reinforcement. He created new environments where people would experiment, reach out, and take risks. His participants were the congregation for the country preacher in him, the restless masses responding to a missionary message. The nation's readers made an author of him; the listeners made a philosopher of him.

Through the years, he experimented, explored new techniques, and added different experiences. He was a perfectionist who never stopped trying to improve the course. He threw away what did not work, while holding on to those elements that continued to inspire. The course was not only his creation but his best means of expression. Everything that he wanted to say to people was relayed in the form of a fourteen-week experience. The course was more powerful than any of his speeches, more lasting than any of his books, more meaningful than the total sum of words he borrowed from worldly pundits and philosophers.

For the authors, seeing Dale Carnegie in this light was the key to understanding his character and to understanding the influence that he has had on American society. We state this not to induce anyone to take the course (the graduates of the course are, historically, far more effective promoters than is any advertising), but to explain the scope of the chapters that follow.

In portraying the life and assessing the influence of Dale Carnegie, we discovered that life and influence were inextricably interwoven. He used almost every experience that he had in his life to help develop the course. It was certainly the foundation, the focus, and the major achievement of his lifetime, as well as a legacy for his heirs. To tell the story of his life, we must also describe the legacy.

What you will be reading here has three components. This book describes Dale Carnegie's life. It also gives some snapshots of what occurs during the course—the experiences of students who take the Dale Carnegie Course today. Finally, the book discusses Dale Carnegie's teaching and his influences on current education, psychology, and personal growth and self-help movements.

Understanding the influence that Dale Carnegie continues to have on students in his course as well as the sources of his methods gives a more complete portrait of Dale Carnegie than can be conveyed by the simple facts of his life.

His dynamism, creativity, and energy—the meaning that he gave to the word enthusiasm—live on in his course and in the millions of students, famous and anonymous, who are inheritors of that tradition. In the glare of the public eye, Dale Carnegie may have looked like a cheerful country preacher with a round-the-clock sermon of enthusiasm. But for many of those students—struggling with their fears, their families, their careers, and their lives—Dale Carnegie has become a friend and a lasting influence.

CHAPTER 1

FLOODS, FRUGALITY, AND FAITH

F OR SKINNY, PALE DALE CARNEGIE, THE PIG-FARMER'S
son in his worn, tightly stretched jacket
and trousers, there was no shortcut to distinction at Warrensburg, Missouri, State Teachers College. Unlike most of the male
campus heroes, who were primarily athletes, Dale showed no
signs of physical prowess. Recalling a self-assured Chautauqua
speaker he had heard, he concluded that he might be able to
prove himself with his speaking ability.

Fortunately, the students at the college held debating and
public-speaking contests in high regard. Dale observed that the
men who won them "were regarded as the intellectual leaders
in college." The public-speaking events drew crowds from the

town as well as the college, and the names of the champions were well known.

With his mother's encouragement, Dale had given a number of speeches in Sunday school. He had also gained some stage experience in high school by playing the role of Snooks, the newsboy, in a play entitled *Imogene*, or *The Witch's Secret*.

"Poor as I was," he recalled, "I had discovered that I could at least stand up and speak with a little more vitality and enthusiasm than the average speaker."

But speaking champions at Warrensburg State Teachers College were not made overnight. First, the contestant had to join a society. Then, only by winning all the contests within his or her society could a speaker become eligible for the intersociety contest.

Carnegie entered a dozen contests—and lost them all.

"After the last one," he later told an audience, "I was ... crushed, ... beaten, ... despondent." His despondency undoubtedly proceeded from a vision of leading a life as hard and grueling as his mother and father's. The family was now living on a new farm where their fortunes were not flourishing any more than in the past.

Dale had little hope for the future. In class, he felt himself an object of ridicule, too embarrassed by his gawky appearance and shabby clothes to concentrate on his work. He saw himself as a social outcast, shunned by young women. More than the mere three miles between the farm and the college separated him from the circle of students who boarded in town. A barrier of poverty stood between him and the others. If he didn't succeed at Warrensburg, Dale might end up following in his father's footsteps. What could be worse than spending the rest of his life as a poverty-stricken Missouri farmer?

There seemed to be no way out.

When he talked about that episode of despair in a speech thirty years later, Carnegie characteristically made light of it by saying, "No, I didn't get out the old shotgun, or anything of that kind, but I literally thought of suicide." Although the comment brought laughs from his audience, Carnegie was serious. Sixteen-year-old Dale took the prospect of failure very hard. After some soul-searching, he had resolved, "There's nothing to that; I'm going to keep on until I win one of those contests!" Each night, he devoted some of his study time to memorizing the words of Abraham Lincoln and Richard Harding Davis. On his rides to and from college he declaimed the speeches he had learned the night before.

A year later, Dale Carnegie won the schoolwide declamatory contest with "The Boy Orator of Zapata" by Davis and Lincoln's "Gettysburg Address." He also made the college record books: Dale noted that he was "the only boy in the history of the college who had ever won the contest away from the girls."

In addition, he won the debating contest, securing for himself the prominent position in student affairs that he had been seeking. Not only did students now recognize his name, they also sought him out for public speaking lessons. Of course, there were a number of girls among those who took lessons from him.

For Carnegie, his college triumph in public speaking was a new beginning. Where he had previously been a social failure conspicuous primarily for his separateness from the other students, he was now regarded as an intellectual leader.

"The last year I was in college," he recalled, "I won the debating contest; the boy I trained won the public-speaking contest; and the girl I trained won the declamatory contest."

Dale could shed his concerns about girls who turned down his buggy rides and boys who laughed behind his back when he stood at the blackboard. The public-speaking connection gave him a way around all the social graces he lacked. Now, instead of seeking out other students, they came to him.

"When I got out of college," he was to remark later, "the only thing I knew I could do probably a little better than some people was training people to speak effectively."

But that talent, alone, proved to be his ticket out of the Missouri farmlands.

THE FAMILY

Harmony Church, the town where Carnegie was born on November 24, 1888, was just a crossroads with a church on the broad flood plain near the 102 River, about ten miles northeast of Maryville, in northwestern Missouri. His first memories were of a two-story, white frame farmhouse with outbuildings at the back and side.

He was born Dale Carnagey. Although Dale's father, James, claimed a remote link to Andrew Carnegie, the steel magnate and philanthropist, any connection is unlikely. Dale himself never claimed, publicly or privately, any relationship to the millionaire Carnegie. When he changed the spelling of his last name, it was clearly for business reasons.

The family moved several times while Dale was growing up. The first move was from Harmony Church to Bedison, when he was five. The second, about the time he was twelve, was to the Ira Moore farm, one mile south of Harmony Church. The final move, to Warrensburg, Missouri, about fifty miles south of Kansas City, occurred in 1904 when Dale was sixteen. The farm near Warrensburg was some three miles from the town and the state teachers college. The college was the equivalent of an advanced high school or junior college. Students from Missouri headed toward careers in teaching could attend tuition-free, paying only room and board. The purpose of that final move during his teenage years was to make it possible for Dale to attend Warrensburg State, while sparing his family the cost of boarding him at the school.

Dale had one sibling, an older brother, Clifton. In later years, he rarely mentioned Cliff. Although they started school together, the boys were never very close. Those who knew Cliff as an adult regarded him as something of a ne'er-do-well. Always motivated and ambitious, Dale would remain frustrated by Cliff's lack of drive. In later years, while Carnegie was building himself a nationwide reputation, Cliff had trouble holding a job of any kind. It was especially galling to Carnegie that his brother moved back to his parents' house and became partially dependent on them when they were aging. Although he tried to motivate his brother and sometimes helped support him, he was dismayed and often annoyed by what he saw as flaws in his brother's character.

FLOODS AND FRUGALITY, POVERTY AND CHARITY

The Carnageys stumbled their way through years of desperate poverty. Dale did not exaggerate when he recalled, years later, how the family strove to make ends meet. Like most Missouri farmers, the Carnageys had varying numbers of milk cows, beef cattle, and pigs. The main cash crops were wheat and corn. The river that had helped create the rich farmland that produced verdant crops rose almost every fall to wreak havoc on those farmers who tried to draw a living from the soil. Year after year, the crops flourished. The wheat and corn ripened. And then the rains came. Days before harvest, the brown waters of the 102 River surged over their banks to engulf the Carnagey fields. The brown tide renewed the soil but destroyed the crops that sprang from it.

Six years out of seven, summer's end brought the same spectacle to the skinny boy with patched and tattered clothes. Standing on the slight rise outside the farmhouse, Dale watched the water creep across the fields. Almost imperceptibly at first, then in a sudden, sweeping torrent that spread across the low-lying plain, the water drowned the roots of the still-waving wheat and crumbled the heavily weighted cornstalks.

The aftermath became as familiar as the annual spectacle of destruction. After the water receded, he would struggle with his father across the muddy field to reclaim whatever stalks had escaped the tide. The family would go into debt again. Again, there would be no money for new clothes. While Dale's mother went about her chores resolutely singing hymns, James Carnagey's face became increasingly grim.

For all his industrious enterprise, James William Carnagey was a man consistently down on his luck. One year when his fields escaped the perennial floods, he managed to harvest a bumper corn crop. He bought feed cattle, fattened them with corn, and sold them for slaughter. But thousands of farmers throughout the Midwest must have been doing the same, for prices plummeted on the Chicago market. The Carnageys made a net profit of thirty dollars for a year's work.

If James Carnagey was a failure as a farmer, it was not for any want of persistence. When the crops and cattle continued to lose money, he began raising mules. But it took three years to raise a mule and break it before you could ship it for sale to Memphis, Tennessee. At the end of three years, the Carnageys had lost money.

Prize hogs were another product of the Carnagey farm, but this venture too ended in disaster. "Year after year," Dale recalled, "our hogs died of cholera and we burned them. I can close my eyes now and recall the pungent odor of burning hog flesh."

Flooded crops; fattened cattle that brought only a few dollars' profit; hogs that had to be incinerated—the parade of disasters would have been comic if it had not spelled such hardship for the family. There was the day Dale's father bought a jackass and led it home to the barn. The jackass stepped on the end of a loose board studded with long nails, which sent the other end of the board, nails and all, through its stomach. It died on the spot.

Despite their poverty, James and Amanda Carnagey always found something to give away to charity, probably at the insistence of Amanda and with the encouragement of the local pastor. The recipient of their gifts was an orphanage, The Christian Home, in Council Bluffs, Iowa. Years later, when Dale would send home a check at Christmastime, he discovered that this, too, went for charity. His parents were helping out a widowed mother who was struggling to take care of her children.

SCHOOL DAYS

A skinny, underfed, towheaded, sensitive boy with big ears and a dimpled chin, young Dale Carnagey was the image of a Tom

Sawyer. He, too, pulled his share of pranks. One winter he brought a dead rabbit to school in a bucket and set it on the potbellied stove when no one was looking. When the fumes eventually reached the teacher, she quickly discovered the culprit. She punished Dale, but the episode significantly improved his reputation among his classmates.

The one-room schoolhouse serving Nodaway County was No. 128, Rose Hill School, about a mile from his farm. For Dale, winter was synonymous with wet, cold feet. He recalled that he had no rubbers or overshoes before the age of fourteen. He walked to and from school through snowdrifts, leaning against the frigid Missouri wind.

Accompanying him on his one-mile walk to Rose Hill rural school were Maude Evans, her younger sister, May, and her brothers Guy, Floyd, Roy, and Glen. Maude remembers Dale as a jolly, popular boy who never worried too much about his studies. But it was her sister, May, whom Dale called his first girlfriend. They had picnics in Coulters Wood near the creek and called each other sweethearts.

Small events centered on the town held enormous importance for this farmboy. In a letter written forty years later, Carnegie recalled, "I can remember, as a child, how we used to do the chores and then hitch up the team and drive over rough, frozen roads to Maryville to attend the Methodist Episcopal church. Mother taught a Sunday school class and we stayed for Class Meeting afterwards and then drove home through the cold." Dinner was at three or four o'clock in the afternoon.

Family members were often reminded of their state of poverty, and throughout those years Dale harbored deep and abiding feelings about his condition.

"Those days," he recalled later, "I was ashamed of the fact that I had to live on the farm—I was ashamed of our poverty; and people who lived in Maryville gave me an inferiority complex."

The Missouri dust, storms, and floods had proved too much for some of the settlers. A number of log cabins stood empty near the Carnagey homestead. Dale and his friends would play in these deserted cabins, climbing up to the attic and jumping to the ground through an open window. One day when he was playing with his friends, Dale gripped the window frame, planted his feet on the sill, and jumped.

A ring on his left forefinger caught on a nail head, but it was too late to stop his fall. As Dale plummeted to the ground, his forefinger was torn off. He screamed in pain, fearing he was going to die, as blood poured from the open wound.

After the bleeding stopped, the wound healed without infection. In later years, Dale said he completely forgot about his injury. But during his school and college years, having only had three fingers and a thumb on his left hand was an additional reason for feeling self-conscious.

THE NARROW VIEW

The provincialism of the farm life Dale Carnegie experienced is difficult to imagine today, but a few of his memories give a clear view of his circumscribed world. At the age of twelve, his biggest thrill was riding with his father in a lumber wagon to Maryville once or twice a month. He recalled there were hitching racks all around the square. After hitching the team, his father would turn to him and hand him a dime "to spend in whatever way I wished."

Another big event was the trip he took with his father to St. Joseph when he was thirteen. James was sending a carload of fattened hogs to the slaughterhouse in the city, and as a special bonus he got two free railroad passes. Dale went along for the ride.

St. Joseph was a city of 60,000—at least a dozen times bigger than the largest town Dale had ever seen. Six-story buildings looked like skyscrapers to him. He watched in amazement as a streetcar went rattling past with its bell ringing.

After delivering the hogs and seeing some of the sights around town, Dale and his father took the train back to Ravenwood, Missouri. They arrived at two o'clock in the morning. It was another four miles back to the farm. Dale was so excited by the day's events that he had been unable to sleep during the train ride. He was ready to drop by the time they arrived home. Somehow he made it, but he later claimed that he walked those four miles in his sleep.

Outsiders were a source of wonder. One of these was Nicholas M. Souder, a teacher who boarded with the Carnageys after they moved to Warrensburg. Mr. Souder won Dale's admiration when he showed the boy his typewriter and adding machine, the first of these instruments that Dale had ever seen. Mr. Souder also held lengthy discussions with the boy, and it was from this boarder that Dale recalled having first heard the words *intuitive* and *psychology*. Both, to him, were impressive words, and he must have hungered for more of Nicholas Souder's wisdom on the subjects. Unfortunately, Mr. Souder lived with the family for only a short time, and after he moved, Dale never heard from him again.

Another event in young Dale's life served to broaden his range of vision. Again, it illustrates just how narrow his world was as a boy. When two trains collided on a siding near Warrensburg, Dale went along with his father to help pull passengers out of the wreck. He got into a conversation with one man, slightly injured, who said he was from Philadelphia.

"So that's how people in Pennsylvania look," Dale remembered thinking. "Shoot, they don't look any different than the people right here in Missouri."

FAITH AND MORALITY

For his mother and father, Dale Carnegie harbored his deepest affection. He often used their lives as examples of the power of courage and strong endurance. Amanda Elizabeth (Harbison) Carnagey was a devout Methodist who wanted both of her sons to become missionaries, ministers, or schoolteachers. She herself had been a country schoolteacher before marrying James Carnagey, a farmhand. Dale's father had only six years of education. Mrs. Carnagey set great store in education as well as religion, and she was the stronger influence in Dale's childhood and early career.

Amanda had strict moral principles and high standards. In

accordance with Methodist doctrine of that era, she allowed no liquor in the house and did not allow her sons to attend dances before the age of fourteen. She once caught him playing with a pack of cards. Snatching the cards from him, she threw them into the fire. For the rest of his life, Carnegie would remember her words: "I would rather hear the clods of earth rattling down on your coffin than to see you soil yourself with such filthy pawns of the devil." Although he did play cards as an adult, it was never without some pangs of guilt.

His first experiences in public speaking came from his mother's side. "Speaking gave me a feeling of importance," he was to recall, "and it was my mother who first trained me."

The church and temperance movement heavily influenced that training. At the Methodist Episcopal church that the Carnageys attended, Amanda would go down on her knees and pray aloud.

After she heard one of Carry Nation's powerful calls to temperance, Amanda Carnagey became a vocal spokeswoman for the cause. She gained a reputation for making speeches about "sin, liquor, and the salvation of souls."

From the way Carnegie described his parents in later years, it is apparent that his hard-working father was sustained through many of his darkest hours by the staunch religious convictions of Dale's mother. Residents of Warrensburg recall that Mrs. Carnagey was always a leader of hymn singing and prayers at the church. Dale never forgot the hymns that she sang as she worked around the house:

> Peace, peace, wonderful peace,
> Flowing down from the Father above,
> Sweep over my spirit forever I pray
> In fathomless billows of love.

Her religious faith was a sustaining force in the Carnagey household. James, on the other hand, was prone to fits of depression when the chores, the mounting debts, and the accumulation of disasters proved almost too much for him.

In *How to Stop Worrying and Start Living*, published in 1948, several years after his father's death, Dale wrote:

> I often heard my mother say that when Father went to the barn to feed the horses and milk the cows, and didn't come back as soon as she expected, she would go out to the barn, fearing that she would find his body dangling from the end of a rope.

A particularly bad spell occurred around 1898, when the Carnagey family was still on the farm outside Maryville. At the age of forty-seven, James Carnagey suffered what today would be called a nervous breakdown. With the debts, the grinding toil, discouragement, and worry, his health finally began to suffer. He stopped eating and became severely emaciated. The family doctor predicted he would be dead within six months.

This was about the time Dale's father paid a visit to the banker in Maryville to plead for more time. The banker threatened to foreclose on the Carnagey property. On the way home, as he crossed the bridge over the 102 River, James Carnagey got off his wagon. He stood peering over the rail into the depths of the river, debating whether he should drown himself or go home.

Dale was a grown man before he learned from his father what had happened that day. "He told me, with tears in his eyes, that if it had not been for mother's religious faith, he would not have had the courage to live through those terrible years."

The contrast between his mother's optimistic faith and his father's dogged fatalism eventually led Dale to believe that neither sort of life provided the answers he was seeking. He was, instead, fascinated by his glimpses of a world that lay far outside the midwestern farming communities. He glimpsed this world in passing when Mr. Souder described the wonders of adding machines and typewriters and when a man from the Philadelphia told him what life was like in a bustling eastern city.

CHAUTAUQUA INSPIRATION

While still in high school, Dale encountered another visitor from the outside world who probably exercised a still greater influence in determining the future course of his life. The man was a Chautauqua speaker.

The Chautauqua movement, begun in 1873 in Chautauqua, New York, was a late nineteenth-century form of adult education classes liberally laced with doses of religion. The movement itself was the brainchild of John Heyl Vincent, a Methodist bishop from Tuscaloosa, Alabama. He believed that secular education should be combined with religious education in a Sunday school class atmosphere that would draw adults as well as children.

Vincent's views on education were shared by Lewis Miller, a friend from Akron, Ohio, who was a small-time inventor and manufacturer as well as a Methodist Sunday school superintendent. In 1874, Vincent and Miller launched a two-week summer training course called The Sunday School Teachers Assembly at the camp meeting ground at Fair Point on Lake Chautauqua. The courses were immensely popular—Vincent and Miller were ardent promoters—and by 1878 the "Chautauqua courses" were being widely attended by the general public. Teachers, preachers, and orators were brought to Chautauqua to deliver courses on literature, science, and religion. In what became the forerunner of correspondence courses, Vincent prescribed a four-year course of reading that enabled students to take examinations and earn a diploma, all while studying at home.

By 1882, more than fifty branches of Vincent and Miller's "Chautauqua Literary and Scientific Circle" had sprung up around the country, while "chautauqua" became the generic term for any sort of educational assembly. At the local chautauquas, lecture programs were both entertaining and instructive —but a tone of moral uplift was sustained throughout. The skillful combination of entertainment and education with religiosity made the chautauquas especially popular in rural areas and small towns. "Daughter assemblies" were held as five- to seven-day events in tents or public halls, and entire families often attended. For many young people, a chautauqua was the first contact with any form of education beyond the local school-house.

The chautauqua speaker witnessed by Dale made a lasting impression on him. Not only was the speaker a world traveler, an outsider visiting the town of Maryville, Missouri, he was also a man who had the power to mesmerize an audience with his eloquence. The subject of his discourse that evening is unknown. It seems certain, though, that the speaker inspired Dale Carnegie to believe that he too could rise above a farming existence. In the manner of speakers on that circuit, the chautauqua lecturer captivated his audience with "the story of a poor farm boy who saw nothing ahead of him but years of dull toil."

"And who would that little boy be?" the orator inquired. "Ladies and gentlemen, you are looking at him!"

Although the scene is reminiscent of the rainmaker coming to call, it is also a reminder of the power that outsiders exercised. They came to tell Americans, in small towns throughout the heartland, of the mysteries and the vast opportunities that lay just beyond their doorsteps.

WORRIES AND FEARS

Throughout his childhood and teenage years, Dale continued to be beset by worries. As he would later recall, many of his childhood concerns focused on the fear of dying. Like many children, he was afraid of thunder and lightning—naturally enough, given the pyrotechnic displays that sometimes occurred over the Missouri farmlands.

And from his Sunday school education came the conviction that he had committed a variety of sins and would eventually be punished for them. Even as a young boy, he feared that he would go to hell when he died. His childhood years were haunted by the fear of being buried alive. When his mother had warned him, shrilly, that she would rather see him in his grave than using playing cards, young Dale had taken the message to heart. The terrible image of being buried beneath the earth occasionally made him burst into tears without warning.

In the school yard, Dale was subjected to a considerable teasing about his prominent, wide ears. One older boy named Sam White tormented him unmercifully and on more than one occasion threatened to cut off Dale's ears. Dale took the threat seriously. Years later, he could still remember the name of the tormentor who had caused him many sleepless nights.

As adolescence approached, it brought with it the usual insecurities about meeting and talking to girls. Although there is no evidence that Dale was ever at a loss for words, the idea of being speechless terrified him. At this age, just thinking about a wedding day frightened him. Recalling his fear, he wrote, "I imagined that we would be married in some country church, and then get in a surrey with the fringe on the top and ride back to the farm . . ."

After that, his mind went blank. He could not imagine what he would say on the ride back to the farm. "How," he asked, "would I be able to keep the conversation going?"

Obviously the preadolescent farm boy plodding along behind his plow worried about more than conversation with his future wife. His understandable sexual anxiety was translated into a palpable fear of being left speechless by the event. Given the religious atmosphere of his upbringing, Carnegie naturally presumed that marriage would be his sexual initiation—that is, assuming any girl would marry him.

In his worst moments, however, he doubted he would ever get as far as making a proposal. As he would later confess to the world in *How to Stop Worrying and Start Living*, "I worried for fear girls would laugh at me if I tipped my hat to them."

TEACHERS COLLEGE

In 1904, when the family moved to Warrensburg, Dale had become, if anything, even more self-conscious about the poverty that burdened his family, hanging around their necks like a yoke.

Undoubtedly, it was Mrs. Carnagey's idea for Dale to go to Warrensburg State Teachers College, with the hope that he would become a teacher, missionary, or minister.

Being within three miles of the college meant that Dale could live at home and ride a horse to class every day. Room-and-board expenses in Warrensburg, somewhere between fifty cents and a dollar a day, were far more than the family could have met. Dale was extremely conscious that he was one of four students—out of a student population of eight hundred—who were so poor that they lived at home and rode to school on horseback.

He had responsibilities on the farm, too. Every morning, he rode his horse to town, attended classes, then galloped back to the farm in time for evening chores. After milking cows, cutting wood, and slopping the hogs, he studied his lessons "by the light of a coal oil lamp," as he dramatically put it.

Even when he climbed into bed, his chores were not finished. James Carnagey, in his endless quest for a productive line of farming, had got into the business of raising valuable, pedigreed, Duroc Jersey hogs. One drawback to raising these hogs was that the sows gave birth in February, when the temperature outdoors was typically well below freezing. To keep the piglets from freezing to death they were kept in a basket covered with a gunny sack located behind the kitchen stove. It was Dale's responsibility to look after them.

> The last thing I did before I went to bed at night was to take that basket of pigs from behind the kitchen stove out to the hog shed, wait for them to nurse, and then bring them back and put them behind the stove. Then I went to bed, and set the alarm for three o'clock; when the alarm went off, I got out of bed in that bitter cold, dressed, took the pigs out for another hot meal, brought them back, set the alarm for six o'clock, and then got up to study my Latin verbs.

If Dale's home life was his private burden, the clothes he wore to class were his visible badge of poverty. His jacket and trousers were always too tight and too short. He told his mother that when he stood at the blackboard to attack a problem in mathematics, he couldn't even think of the problem—"I can only think of the fact that people are probably laughing at my clothes."

Dale's mother assured him that she would like to buy him better clothes, but it was impossible. The Carnageys simply couldn't afford it.

The final disgrace (and undoubtedly the worst, since he remembered it for decades) was the moment when he asked Patsy Thurber to go buggy-riding with him. Patsy was one of the most attractive girls at the college. Like most of the other students from around Missouri, she lived at the college. She seemed friendly. Occasionally, she waved to Dale as he rode into town on horseback. Once, she asked him to explain an assignment to her.

Finally, Dale mustered his courage. One day after class, he caught up with her as she was leaving the building. He asked her to go buggy-riding with him the following Sunday. Without a moment's hesitation, she turned him down.

That day, during his long ride from the college to the farm, Dale made a promise to himself he would keep. Someday he would distinguish himself so thoroughly that the girl who turned him down would be proud to associate with him.

MEMORIES OF CHILDHOOD

In the early sessions of the Dale Carnegie Course today, students talk about childhood experiences. Some have nostalgic memories, like those Carnegie often repeated about his Missouri boyhood. Others tell about painful or pleasant growing experiences. Everyone can remember an accident, some slight or indignity, the excitement of an important moment, or a minor triumph.

Carnegie realized that this opportunity was important for everyone in the course. For him, public speaking had been a way to excel. In his course, others get the same chance.

During a recent course meeting in a large conference room in a downtown hotel, thirty-four men and women are listening to the twenty-six-year-old manager of a computer store. He is at

once restless and energetic. He talks in a fast-paced, stacc
style. Unconsciously, he keeps hitching up the waist of his t
sers. As his enthusiasm increases, the corduroys start slip
down again. He resembles a seven-year-old at an amuser
park, waiting breathlessly for his turn at the Beanbag Toss

He has wild, curly blonde hair. A pair of wire-rim glasse
persistently down his nose. As he speaks to the audience, he
stops, turns and paces, stops again. His words come out ra

> I'm from a small town about ninety miles from here
> very small town. You've never heard of it. My father we
> in the steel plant—or he did until it shut down. I've
> four brothers. They all stayed home, so everyone in
> family assumed I would stay home, too. But I always l
> I wanted to go to college. I didn't say anything to my pai
> but I knew I wanted to go to college. The way they le
> it, that's like betraying them, because none of my bro
> would do that. My brothers are just going to stay the
> work like my father. So . . .

He stops, hitches his pants, pushes up his glasses.

> So one night I told my mother and father after I gr
> I was going to college. I'm the oldest. They didn't
> I could do that. I was deserting them. My mot
> mother doesn't get mad—but she got mad. She sai
> a traitor, you're deserting us. Get out of here. I d
> you to spend another night in this house."
> My father doesn't show anything. But this nigh
> forget. He was sitting in front of the TV. I packed
> I just threw some things in a bag, because I knew
> meant it—she didn't want me to spend anotl
> that house. So I had my bag and as I walked pa
> he turned from the TV and looked at me and
> tears in his eyes, and he said, "How could ye
> us?"
> So I left. And I'm walking to my friend's ho
> know I can stay there. It's five miles and I'm

I've only got a light jacket on because that's all I took, and I'm thinking to myself, "Did I do the right thing? Did I do the right thing? Did I do the right thing?" And I'm thinking to myself, "They don't want me to leave, but I have to do it. I have to." And I was right.

In the back of the room, the electric timer on a wrist watch emits a high-pitched "beep-beep-beep." A voice calls out "Twenty seconds!"

The speaker pushes up his glasses and begins pacing again, picking up the pace:

So I went to live with my friend and finished high school and went to college, and then I got this job. I'm doing very well, I'm store manager, and I think in another month I'll be general manager. For a long time, I couldn't go back, but then I did. The last time I was home, I heard my mom talking to a neighbor about me, telling our neighbor how proud she was that I graduated from college. And I could really hear the pride in her voice.

I don't have to worry, because I did what I told myself I had to do then because it was right for me. Now here I am, I'm successful, and my mom's happy, I know she is, and I know that wouldn't have happened if I'd just stayed there and done what they wanted me to. So my point is, do what you think is right, and you'll feel good about yourself.

"Two minutes!" calls the voice from the back of the room. Thirty-four people applaud. The speaker darts into an empty air, sits down, and pushes his glasses high on his nose.

SELF-CONFIDENCE AND SELF-ESTEEM

oday's psychologists draw a distinction between self-confidence and self-esteem. Typically, self-confidence is how you feel

about a particular skill or about your ability to handle a particular situation. Self-esteem, on the other hand, is a more fundamental feeling that you have about yourself. Self-esteem is what you feel you are worth, what you feel you deserve, regardless of your skills or faults.

When Dale Carnegie began teaching his course, the transformation that he saw taking place in people was what he called "developing self-confidence." Pragmatist that he was, Dale Carnegie looked for the physical, outward displays of self-confidence before anything else. He decided that anyone who overcame the initial shakes to stand up and give a speech in public was well on his way to achieving self-confidence.

But many of the over 150,000 people who take the Dale Carnegie Course every year already have self-confidence. That is, many are reasonably good and successful at what they do. They have confidence in their own ability to run a computer, deliver a product, analyze a management problem, present a case before a jury, write a report, or design a suspension bridge. But for all their abilities in performing specific skills and solving particular problems, they may still be lacking in self-esteem.

How do we lose self-esteem? How do successful people manage to make their way to high places with their abilities intact but their self-image damaged by slights, wounds, or even devastating injuries?

The fact is, most of our lives are not full of praise or encouragement. From the kindergarten playground to the high school locker room, from the fraternity suite to the university club, from the business lunch to the barroom floor, one of the most common ways we express friendship or camaraderie is with sarcasm or put-downs. Professionally, most organizations and most managers are not oriented toward positive reinforcement. Even our educational process, for most people, focuses on reminding us of our shortcomings—measured by the distance we fall short of achieving an A or a 4.0 rather than the mental strides we have successfully taken to arrive where we are.

Even if we do find the praise and encouragement we need at one level of accomplishment, we may find ourselves lacking the self-esteem that we need in order to reach the next level. Self-esteem makes us feel we *deserve* more. It motivates us to *move* toward our goals.

The self-esteem that Dale experienced as a result of a double win in the declamatory and debate contests contributed directly to his self-confidence in teaching other students how to do it. He marveled, "Then, other people came to me for training in public speaking—I, mind you, who had been through a series of devastating, continued defeats!"

Suddenly, the defeats didn't matter. At Warrensburg State Teachers College, one win was enough to clear his record. Two in a row secured his self-confidence. That is, as long as his ability to speak in public held out, so would the sense of feeling good about himself that went with it. The student who had been unable to win even a single contest in his own society was now the most sought-after teacher. His performance improved to meet expectation. He not only *saw* himself as being capable of teaching others, but by seeing himself in that light, he *was* capable.

When a student today stands up in a Dale Carnegie course session to tell anything about his or her life, the class always greets that person with a round of applause. By telling his or her own story, that person wins automatic and unqualified approval. It takes a certain self-confidence to tell the story. But the result—what comes with the applause at the end of that short speech—is heightened self-esteem.

What Carnegie observed in those students he taught was precisely what he had seen happen to himself. Once you are on a cycle of success, you will continue to expect more of yourself. You will want to *build* on each success. As you do, you may find that your self-esteem sometimes needs shoring up. But you can accomplish that, yourself, by setting a series of definite goals that you meet, either in the context of a group or class, or else on your own.

Anyone who has observed a number of Dale Carnegie classes begins to note an interesting statistical phenomenon. Out of a class of thirty-five or forty students, during a fourteen-week period perhaps eight or nine will report promotions, new jobs, or going into business for themselves.

Of course, the sample found in Dale Carnegie courses is not really representative of the general population. Most of the course members want to get ahead, to succeed, or to change their lives in some way. That's probably why they join the course in the first place. Nonetheless, that they do act *during* that four-teen-week period is significant.

Carnegie would say this happens because the course allows students to conquer their fear of public speaking, to feel better about themselves. They become more capable of achieving what-ever they decide is important to them.

After all, if it worked for a callow Missouri farmboy, why shouldn't it work for anyone?

CHAPTER 2

THE LURE
OF SELLING

I N 1908, THE YEAR DALE CARNEGIE LEFT COLLEGE, America was in the middle of an unparalleled explosion of economic growth and free enterprise. Although western Missouri farmers like James Carnagey were still wrestling with crop failures, animal sickness, droughts, storms, and floods, the rest of America was in the midst of a boom.

Sixteen years after making his first motorcar, Henry Ford was selling tens of thousands of Model T's "for business or for pleasure," as his ads stated. Electric lights were beginning to glow in the homes of ordinary citizens of modest means. With indoor plumbing, you no longer had to trek out to the shack with the half-moon on the door in the middle of winter.

Annual sales at J. C. Penney's many Golden Rule Stores were

approaching the $2 million mark. A&P stores formed a chain from Boston to Milwaukee, and Frank W. Woolworth was selling "Five and Ten-Cent Goods, Specialties, Etc.," for cash only, throughout the East. Remington was bragging about "a steadily rising tide of popularity and success," boosted by his recent huge sale of typewriters to the firm of Dun, Barlow and Company (predecessor to Dun and Bradstreet).

With the help of "The N.C.R. Primer—How I Sell a Cash Register," by supersalesman Joseph H. Crane, National Cash Register was sending hundreds of salesmen on the road. They were thoroughly prepared to recite a canned presentation, word for word. George Eastman had created a vast dealer organization to sell cameras to an eager buying public. Gardiner G. Hubbard was pushing the invention of his brilliant son-in-law, Alexander Graham Bell, as hard as he knew how. Inspired by such pioneers in marketing as Morris Robinson, thousands of life-insurance agents were making door-to-door calls. R. W. Sears had teamed up with A. C. Roebuck to go head-to-head with the mail-order business of Aaron Montgomery Ward, while Rowland Hussey Macy and John Wanamaker perfected their individualistic concepts of department store merchandising. The first shopping center, Roland Park Shopping Center, five miles north of Baltimore, opened in 1907.

To a young man stepping off the windblown campus of a western Missouri teacher's college, the opportunities awaiting the salesman were far vaster than any promises buried in the soil. Carnegie discovered that one of his classmates, Frank Self, had spent a summer selling courses for the Denver branch office of International Correspondence Schools. Frank told Carnegie that he had made $20 a week, plus expenses, and Carnegie took him at his word. A vision of unimaginable riches opened before his eyes. Twenty dollars was more than Carnegie's father made in a whole month of work on the farm.

Failing Latin, Carnegie never graduated from Warrensburg State Teachers College, but he had made up his mind that he did not want to become a schoolteacher. In 1908, bright prospects awaited him. He was eager to be out in the world, sharing in America's tide of prosperity. He headed straight to Denver, knocked on the door of the regional sales office of International Correspondence Schools, and asked for a job as salesman.

They hired him on the spot.

THE DRIVE TO SUCCEED

It is tempting to portray twenty-year-old Dale Carnegie as a brash, enthusiastic young man determined to make his way in the world. There are a number of reasons, however, to doubt that he faced this particular challenge with an ever-sunny disposition.

He mixed a drive to succeed with the almost certain conviction that he had already, at this young age, failed to fulfill his mother's ambitions. During his childhood he had been acutely conscious that she wanted him to pursue some line of teaching or religious work. For a while he thought seriously of becoming a foreign missionary.

In college, however, he experienced a crisis of faith that may have been the result of his first encounter with Darwinism. He took courses in biology and other sciences, as well as philosophy and comparative religion. Some dozen years before the Scopes trial, theories of evolution propounded by Darwin were being studied for the first time in many schools. It was a shock for a Bible-trained schoolboy to learn of the theory that the human race did not in fact proceed from Adam and Eve in the Garden of Eden.

In a comparative religion class Carnegie studied the sources of the Bible. He began to regard it as a book of stories the truth of which, in many cases, was doubtful. This realization, too, left him feeling helpless and disoriented, as if the roots of his faith had been torn away.

Three decades later, he was eloquent on the impact of this education:

I didn't know what to believe. I saw no purpose in life. I stopped praying. I became an agnostic. I believed that all

life was planless and aimless. . . . I sneered at the idea of a
beneficent God who had created man in His own likeness.

Although Carnegie would later regain a measure of his faith,
he was still reeling from the shock of disillusionment when he
left teachers college. Life seemed emptier once he began ques-
tioning the existence of an all-seeing Deity. No more did he feel
as if God looked after every sparrow's fall. It was, instead, every
man for himself.

Nor could Carnegie turn to his father for the moral support
he needed. Bogged down in his troubles at the farm, never es-
caping the deadening round of chores, James was not a man to
encourage his son to risk new challenges or dare the world.
Undoubtedly, he joined his wife in hoping that Dale would become educated and find a degree of success his father had never
known. But there is no sign that James inspired his son with
any words of advice or example of courage. As Carnegie headed
for Denver, he was very much on his own.

He was not without resources, however. Since early childhood,
Carnegie had been a tenacious debater. Once he got hold of an
argument, he would not let go.

Persistence was necessary to sell International Correspondence School courses. Carnegie immediately began receiving two
dollars a day for room and board, "plus commissions." He soon
discovered, however, that citizens scattered throughout Nebraska were not eagerly awaiting mail-order education. His one
sale of an International Correspondence course was to a lineman
on a telegraph pole in Alliance, Nebraska. With Carnegie persistently shouting his arguments up the pole, the lineman eventually agreed to sign up for a course in electrical engineering.

Jubilant, Carnegie returned to the regional office to report his
success and receive his commission. But one success could not
make up for many failures, and Carnegie soon began to look
elsewhere. One day, when he was talking to a seasoned salesman
of the National Biscuit Company, Carnegie received some sound
advice. The veteran suggested that Carnegie start selling something for which there was a constant demand. He pointed out

that staple items such as cookies and crackers were always needed by merchants. The National Biscuit Company salesman had made friends with them all. Selling, for him, meant paying each of them a monthly visit, noting what was missing from their inventory, sitting down for a cup of coffee, and turning in his order to NBC.

At the time he met the biscuit salesman, Carnegie was near the end of his resources, both financial and emotional. Expecting to make twenty dollars a week, as his friend Frank Self had bragged of doing, Carnegie was profoundly disappointed to discover that he could not even complete a second sale. What did it mean? Was he destined not to be a salesman? Did he lack courage—or was he doing something wrong? If Frank Self could succeed at International Correspondence School, why couldn't Dale Carnegie?

CROSSROAD

Carnegie had left Warrensburg without looking back, but he now faced a grim choice. Should he go back, finish his education, and become a teacher or foreign missionary, as his mother wanted? Go back to the farm where, he was certain, he would always be needed? In all his weeks with the International Correspondence School he had saved nothing. The two dollars a day that had first seemed so generous was barely enough to get by on. When Carnegie took out for room, board, and travel expenses—which he had to cover out-of-pocket—he had nothing left.

As Carnegie pondered his alternatives, the memory of the bustling stockyards of St. Joseph must have come to mind. At least he knew something about the meat business. Why not work for a meat-packing company? Destination: Omaha, stockyard capital of Nebraska and headquarters of Armour and Company. But Omaha was five hundred miles away by rail, and Carnegie only had enough in his pocket to cover the next meal.

Again recalling the boyhood trip to St. Joe, Carnegie knew that ranchers often needed an extra hand to feed and water the cattle during the journey. He packed his suitcase, handed in his resignation at International Correspondence School and headed for the freight yard. With some persistent inquiries and persuasive arguments—after all, he was an *experienced* hand, even if he looked like a salesman these days—Carnegie wangled himself a free trip to Omaha. In the shuddering freight car, surrounded by cattle, Carnegie wondered what lay at the end of the rail. He had no real prospect of finding a job and nothing in his pocket to guarantee a night's lodging or a square meal.

He was trusting to luck that something would turn up, and as soon as he arrived in Omaha, luck smiled on him. Salesmen were in demand. Carnegie changed his shirt, put on a tie, brushed his jacket and trousers, polished his shoes, and asked the way to the main office of Armour and Company in South Omaha.

One hour later, he had a job. Even more miraculously, he would have a month-long training program before he was sent on the road. Carnegie was very impressed with his new boss, Rufus E. Harris, who signed his name without lifting pen from paper. Then and there, Carnegie made it a practice to begin signing his own name the same way.

His first assignment: the Dakota Territory. Salary: $17.31 per week plus expenses. Since "expenses" included room, board, and travel, Carnegie's new income went straight into his pocket or savings account.

With a mixture of pride and relief, Carnegie sat down at the company boarding house to compose a letter to his mother and father. Several days later he received a reply from his father that included the comment: "$17.31 a week! I don't think Armour and Company can keep it up!"

WILD WEST SALESMAN

Despite the improved income, selling beef to small towns in the Dakotas was not an idyllic existence. In those days, any kind of selling was a hit-or-miss business. You might get the order, but getting paid was another matter. Local merchants often came up empty-handed at the end of the month, then offered to exchange some of their extra wares or local farm goods instead of money.

Lowell Thomas, with whom Carnegie worked closely at times after 1916, would later tell the story of the storekeeper who was unable to pay for the bacon and lard he had ordered from Armour. When Carnegie pressed him for payment, the storekeeper offered a dozen pair of shoes. Carnegie later sold the shoes to local railway workers, then forwarded the correct payment in cash to Armour and Company.

Thomas also stated that Carnegie "studied books on salesmanship," but if that is the case, he must have done very little studying. Salesmanship, in those days, was a field few people had studied, and even fewer had written about. Neophyte salesmen (and they were almost entirely men on the road in those days) learned their lessons via war stories shared with other salesmen at the corner bar.

Many companies, like the Equitable Life Insurance Company, had their own manuals for agents, but these were proprietary collections of information designed primarily to pitch a specific product. Carnegie was one of the fortunate ones who had a training course before he took to the road. More often, the men were provided with some scant information on their product, told their territories, and wished good luck.

Carnegie's territory for Armour was the western area of South Dakota, the long, arid plain stretching from west of the Missouri River to the foot of the Black Hills. Its center—and probably the city where Carnegie sold the most goods—was Rapid City, near the present-day site of Mt. Rushmore. Raising beef cattle was already a major enterprise in South Dakota, and meat-packing plants were being established around the state. But Carnegie offered his customers products they couldn't get from next-door suppliers.

Carnegie's routine would have been to take a few wide swings through the territory every year, traveling by Pullman, then freight train, by stagecoach, and occasionally on horseback. Arriving in town, he would drop in on the local merchant, talk about crops and weather, then bring the conversation around

to the Armour Company and its outstanding reputation for providing lean bacon, gentle soap, and tins of the highest quality
lard. Armour could also offer fresh beef packed in ice, or ham
or pork shipped in barrels of brine, conveniently sliced and pack-
aged for the trade.

"And *why* should you buy from Armour?" he would ask. "I'll
tell you why . . ." and he would praise the excellence of service
and the consistent high quality of his company's product. Then
he gave his personal assurances that deliveries would be on time,
to the customer's complete satisfaction.

The entire pitch was no doubt liberally spiced with stories of
Carnegie's own experiences feeding the pigs and tending the
cattle on his father's farm—and probably with popular quotations from Benjamin Franklin ("A penny saved is a penny
earned") or Abraham Lincoln—all delivered in the twangy, broad
accent of western Missouri. Carnegie's farm background meant
he was someone these South Dakota merchants could trust, not
one of the city slickers who sometimes passed through. His eager
manner, ready smile, and enthusiasm made them ready to do
business with him. And his stubborn persistence meant that he
wouldn't go away until they signed an order.

Once he finished business, Carnegie would dash down to the
station, hoping to catch the last freight out of town before the
sound of its whistle died in the distance. Failing that, he was
forced to spend the night in a dingy hotel room, separated by a
hanging sheet of white muslin from the snoring salesman in the
next bunk. Neither a drinker nor a gambler, Carnegie probably
retired after dining in the saloon. No doubt he carried a few dime
Westerns along with a copy of Elbert Hubbard's *Scrapbook* of
famous sayings. He would read by the light of a gas lamp after
filling out his daily report schedule for Armour and Company,
and would fall asleep to the rumble of voices, shouts of drunken
farmhands, and women's laughter that drifted up from the saloon downstairs.

Before dawn, Carnegie was at the wash basin in stockinged
feet, splashing cold water on his face and fastening on a crisp
new collar to face the day's customers.

By dint of hard work, constant travel, and steady improvement in salesmanship, Carnegie rose to the number one position in his territory.

He impressed his superiors at Armour and Company. Whatever their expectations for him in the beginning, Dale Carnegie had proved that he had what it took to succeed in a very challenging territory.

When Carnegie returned to Omaha, Mr. Harris offered him a management position. Respectfully, Carnegie declined. During his days on the road, he had managed to put away $500. Although the management position was attractive, and he was flushed with his success in selling (a long way from the disaster of the International Correspondence School), Dale Carnegie had already begun to think about going east.

RESTLESS AND DEFIANT

In later years, easterners who met the Dale Carnegie of public-speaking fame were derisive of his slow and easy midwestern manner. Journalists who interviewed the prominent author wondered how such an unassuming individual could have clawed his way up the ladder of success.

Carnegie's actions, especially the decision to go east, were not informed by any great understanding of the world or of American achievers. Nor were his ambitions stated in grandiloquent terms. His gestures, instead, were simple actions. Even more than ambition, a restlessness stirred by a number of warring impulses dictated his behavior.

He was always aware of his mother's expectations of him, yet he would never become the missionary that she wanted him to be. Carnegie had the romantic notion that he could be a powerful orator—a hope based on his success as a Sunday school speaker and a rural college debating champ. If he was to prove himself, he knew he would have to go east. After all, the East was the epicenter of American intellect and talent. There, he planned to study speech and drama, with a view to becoming a Chautauqua speaker—or, better yet, an actor.

In his own low-key manner, he was defying his midwestern

roots as he struggled to find a better place for himself in the world. By all rights, Dale Carnegie should have taken the management position with Armour and Company. There he would have been secure for life. Thousands of other young men were making such choices. Carnegie, however, dreamed of something better. Boston, he had decided, was the place to get ahead. But by the time he left Omaha, his choice of destination had changed.

On one of his train rides across South Dakota, Carnegie had met a passenger calling himself Reverend Russell. When the reverend learned of Carnegie's aspirations, he immediately began dispensing advice.

Reverend Russell considered himself experienced in matters of the theater. He said he had produced numerous plays and taught drama to many famous actors and actresses. Boston was not what Carnegie wanted at all. Carnegie wanted New York. *That* was the heart of the theater world. If Carnegie wanted to make his mark and prove his talents, New York was the place to go.

Carnegie was easily swayed. When he asked the name of the foremost acting school in New York, Reverend Russell recommended the American Academy of Dramatic Arts.

Carnegie remembered this conversation when, months later, he turned down the promotion at Armour and Company, packed his suitcase once again, and headed for the station. He had made up his mind.

"One, please," he said, stepping up to the ticket window, "for New York City."

OUT OF THE RANKS

In session five of the Dale Carnegie Course—which has come to be known as the breaking-through session—there is a phrase that is repeated again and again, first by the class as a whole, and then by each individual who comes to the front of the room. The phrase refers to "people in the ranks" who are going to "stay in the ranks" because they don't have "the ability to get things done." It is accompanied by the rhythmic interjection of a repeated question ("Why?"), and then a forceful declaration ("I'll *tell* you why!").

During the class, the words are repeated like a refrain, first by the whole group, then by individuals who come to the front of the room.

The cumulative effect is cathartic. Repeated again and again, these words take on special meaning for each person in the class. For some, it is an outcry of frustration directed against jobs that may have become dull and repetitious; against stubborn coworkers who stand in the way of innovation, experimentation, and progress; against the feelings of anonymity and inertia that can creep into daily lives.

This session is an anomaly in the Dale Carnegie Course—an opportunity for participants to vent frustration and anger in a classroom setting. But the outburst of expression is carefully controlled by the instructor, who limits each person to a few brief moments on stage.

Seeing participants rant against "people who stay in the ranks," it is hard to imagine easygoing Dale Carnegie, who rarely raised his voice in anger, devising such a cathartic group experience. But he recognized the need for this session as integral to the growth experience that takes place during the course. Loudly and vociferously, each member of the class is making a vehement promise to break *out* of the ranks and *to get things done*.

The script in this session comes straight from Dale Carnegie —and it clearly reflects his own, fervent determination to achieve more than the people "in the ranks" of ordinary life. When he gave up his sales career to pursue acting, Dale Carnegie broke out of the ranks. That was a turning point in his own life. Afterwards, he felt confident telling people *they had the ability to get things done*. To salespeople, especially, this is an important message.

BREAKING THROUGH

For the past ten years, Jim Cary has successfully managed three small, gourmet-style sandwich shops. Jim is tall, thin, with sharply cut features and dark brown eyes. He's always extremely well dressed in hand-tailored Italian suits. Anyone meeting him for the first time would see an apparently self-assured, successful businessman, confident in manner, obviously self-directed and in control.

But during the weeks of the course, class members have come to see another Jim Cary—someone who is highly competent but frustrated in his position, wanting to achieve more but not having a clear direction. He has said this is a critical time in his life. He wants to take advantage of some opportunities. He is sure he has the ability, but he says he lacks confidence.

One evening he stands up in front of the class, folds his hands in front of him, and begins:

> Well, this week I took the plunge. I've been talking to some investors, and we worked out an arrangement. I'm starting my own company. I've sold everything and invested it in the business. I'm a part-owner in it now, and I know there will be hard times, but I think it's going to be successful. You've heard me talk about being nervous before, and I'm still nervous. But when you voted to give me the improvement award in session four, that was very important for me. I know I don't have to be nervous.
>
> When I was talking to my investors, I did a presentation that was very well organized, very professional. I know I impressed them. I gave them confidence that I could do it, my enthusiasm showed. Now I'm very up, I'm very confident, and I'm enthusiastic because I know it's going to work for me. So—thank you. All of you. I'm nervous about this new business, but I'm very happy.

There is applause as Jim sits down. The instructor comes to the front of the class. Briefly, the instructor congratulates Jim and notes how everyone has seen his enthusiasm grow during the past few weeks. He sees Jim's move in a very positive light. The way he has gotten his investors to work with him toward a common goal is a sign that Jim can work with people, can arouse their eager interest, can get them saying "yes." That's the key to successful selling.

LESSONS IN SELLING

During the years that he was building the Dale Carnegie Course in Effective Speaking and Human Relations, Carnegie must have reflected frequently on the mistakes he had made and the lessons he had learned as a traveling salesman from Omaha.

One of the fundamental adages of the Carnegie system continues to challenge every salesperson who is in business today. Although Carnegie must have had a vague formulation of this selling principle based upon his firsthand experiences, he found the clearest expression of it in a book published in 1925, written by a professor at the College of the City of New York.

The book, *Influencing Human Behavior* by Harry Overstreet, was one of the first self-help books based on applied psychology. The principle espoused by Professor Overstreet was straightforward:

> First, *arouse in the other person an eager want*. He who can do this has the world with him. He who cannot walks a lonely way.

This would seem commonplace to most salespeople today. In books, tapes, and training programs, they hear this fundamental principle expressed in a wide variety of forms. But during Carnegie's era it was an idea that went against the usual notion of sales technique.

In the days when salesmen were only a step above peddlers, the art of selling was still the art of pitching your product. The Armour program may have taught Carnegie how to talk a great line—and, if in doubt, how to keep talking until he wore the customer down. Just as Carnegie had treed the electrician on the telegraph pole, the country salesman often cornered the customer. The salesman trapped and held him with an onslaught of verbiage and released him only when he cried, "Enough!" and placed his order.

As Carnegie discovered on the road, this was not always a workable tactic—not when you needed repeat business, and especially not when the customer was obliged to meet with half a dozen or more competing salesmen every day. As America churned out mass products, more and more salesmen appeared at the door. Buyers became shrewder.

Something new was needed—a different human-relations tool. Today, this is termed needs identification. In the parlance of the twenties, it was the arousal of wants.

When it comes to identifying those wants, however, little has changed in the course of decades. Those described recently by psychologist Abraham Maslow bear a close resemblance to the list drawn up by Professor Overstreet in the 1920s. Among high-ranking needs are the following:

- Comfort (and, Maslow would add, sex)
- Affectionate devotion
- Play
- Security
- To own something
- To be efficient
- Social esteem
- Pride in appearance
- Cleanliness

Not only salesmanship but also twentieth-century advertising was adding new impetus to the needs-identification movement. Professor Overstreet, for instance, noticed that advertisers continually appealed to many of the human wants on his list. "The advertiser," he declared, "despite all the hard things we have to say of him, is a pioneer in psychological technique."

What worked in advertising, Carnegie could see, should also work in sales. Paring down Professor Overstreet's principle to the fewest possible words, Carnegie stated it, memorably and permanently, in a phrase that is fundamental to the Dale Carnegie way of selling:

Arouse in the other person an eager want.

Carnegie did more than just present the principle. Looking back on his own career selling bacon and lard in South Dakota, he reflected on what had made him successful as a salesman and what he could have done to improve himself. The merchants had obviously liked his storytelling. When Carnegie made his case for Armour products, he always followed up with a good story. The story would hold their attention. After the story, Carnegie would make his point and describe a benefit. That format, telling a story, delivering a point, and describing a benefit would work for everyone who understood the principle of arousing an eager want.

In Carnegie's view, a salesman had the power to lead someone to action. By describing his own experience, the speaker aroused interest in his listener. By delivering a point, he exhorted the listener to do likewise. By describing a benefit, he showed the listener what would be gained by following the speaker's advice.

But to be effective, the *principle* had to be supported by a *method*. Closely related to his method for delivering public speeches, Carnegie's sales technique was an action program for successful selling, founded on his experiences as a twenty-two-year-old salesman struggling to make a career in the Dakota badlands.

CHAPTER 3

A FARMBOY
IN SHOW
BUSINESS

W HATEVER THE CREDENTIALS OF THE REVEREND
Russell of South Dakota, he was correct
in his appraisal of the American Academy of Dramatic Arts.

Edward G. Robinson (then Emanuel Goldenberg) became a student at the AADA in 1911, just one year after Dale Carnegie. Together with RADA (the Royal Academy of Dramatic Arts, in London), Robinson judged the American Academy of Dramatic Arts to be "the best acting school in the world."

The AADA has a history that throws light on what Carnegie was to learn during his tenure there and then put into practice as both actor and teacher. The school had been founded in 1886 by James Morrison Steele MacKaye, who strove to create a style of acting that was "sincere, natural, and free from artificiality."

Steele MacKaye, through his instructions to classes and private pupils, urged young actors to be more sincere and natural in their speech and gestures. MacKaye wanted actors to produce physical movements that resembled those of real people in real situations. Actors should eliminate the posturing and artificiality often found on the stage.

Through his teaching, MacKaye influenced an entire new generation of actors and actresses. He also inspired the growth of three students who went on to become prominent teachers of speech and acting: Samuel S. Curry, head of the Curry School of Expression; Dr. Charles W. Emerson, head of the Emerson College of Oratory; and Franklin H. Sargent, who became president of the American Academy of Dramatic Arts. The last was the Franklin Sargent who auditioned Carnegie for admission into the Academy.

As a journalist later reported, "Sargent looked Carnegie over and without any other comment commanded him to imitate a chair. Dutifully, he bent his knees and raised his arms to emulate the arms of a chair." Carnegie was admitted on the spot. The entrance fee was $400, which ate up nearly his entire savings.

The audition sounds remarkably casual, but Carnegie may have exaggerated the ease with which he got into the AADA. For Edward G. Robinson (who one day would reach stardom in *Little Caesar*, *Five Star Final*, and *Double Indemnity*), it was a signal achievement to be admitted into the AADA. Robinson pulled strings to get an audition. After waiting months to see Mr. Sargent, he was thrilled to be accepted into the program with a scholarship. Without a moment's hesitation, he dropped out of his junior year of college at New York University just so he could attend the AADA.

Another student of the Academy who entered in 1909, the year before Carnegie, was Howard Lindsay. With Russell Crouse, Lindsay would later write *Arsenic and Old Lace*, *The Sound of Music*, and *Life With Father*, some of the longest-running hits in the history of Broadway. Lindsay gave up an education at Harvard and a career in the ministry to go to the AADA. "It was a rewarding six months," he recalled. "The Academy, oldest and best training school in the country, was excellently run by its founder, Franklin H. Sargent."

Another classmate who would later praise the school was Guthrie McClintic, the distinguished producer and director of such Broadway hits as *Ethan Frome*, *Hamlet* with John Gielgud, and *The Barretts of Wimpole Street*.

Given the general praise of its most successful students and the high regard in which it was held throughout the theater world, the credentials of the Academy seem to have been considerably more important than Carnegie recognized at the time.

He certainly received an excellent education in the fundamentals of acting during the intensive six months that students spent at the school. Classes in reading, movement, fencing, and interpretation were interspersed with instruction in pantomime, voice placement, articulation, history of the theater, and practice in acting for comedy, for "dramatic" theater, and for the modern stage.

While he studied, Carnegie and other actors roomed together in what he would later describe as "a kind of cell in a dismal rooming house in the West Forties."

A NEW SCHOOL
OF ACTING

Two years before Carnegie entered the school, the Academy's longtime director, Charles Jehlinger, issued a statement of the school's principles:

> To create an accent on naturalism accompanied by emotional recall in order to achieve a deeper more essential "truth" in performance.

The stated purpose of the AADA acting program is almost exactly what Carnegie would try to teach in public speaking. It is no coincidence that during his six months in the AADA program, he was thoroughly immersed in methods intended to produce a more naturalistic interpretation and manner of performance.

One of the benefits of the program was that students enrolled in the Academy had a "courtesy to the profession" status and received free admission (albeit for standing room) to most current Broadway shows. During the season of 1910 on Broadway, the fare was mostly light romantic comedies, frothy musicals, overproduced spectacles, and modern melodramas. There were many chic revues and star vehicles.

The young man from the western plains could now sample the glittering, star-studded, suggestive, and slightly sinful aura of Broadway. He could witness Florenz Ziegfeld's *Follies* on a stage atop the New York Theater at Broadway and 45th Street. That show featured the incomparable Anna Held, Florenz's wife—five feet tall, with untold inches of bust line. She was accompanied by a sizzling cast of chorus girls wearing $123,000 worth of costumes. Or he could stand at the rear of Hippodrome and watch a crowd of chorus girls dance across a 116-foot stage, followed closely by George Washington, Benjamin Franklin, Buffalo Bill, Pocahontas, Julius Caesar, Mark Antony, Herod, General Pershing, Louis XIV, the Duke of Wellington, Admiral Schley, Henry VI, Helen of Troy, and Napoleon.

1910 was the season that brought those spectacular unmemorable hits *Get-Rich-Quick Wallingford*, *Alias Jimmy Valentine*, with H.B. Warner and Laurette Taylor, *Madame X*, with Dorothy Donnelly, and *Baby Mine*, with Marguerite Clark and Ernest Glendinning. Among the musicals, Carnegie had his choice of *Madame Sherry*, *Naughty Marietta*, *Alma*, *Where Do You Live?*, *The Spring Maid*, or *The Arcadians*. Ethel M. Barrymore was in *Mid-Channel*. Sarah Bernhardt was on one of her many farewell tours, and Helen Hayes was in *The Summer Widowers* with Lew Fields.

POLLY OF THE CIRCUS

Graduation from the Academy did not, by any stretch of the imagination, guarantee a lead role in a long-running Broadway

hit. Although AADA credentials may have given the young graduates a slight edge, the real test—auditions, auditions, and more
auditions—still lay ahead of these apt young pupils. They had
the talent, they had the skills, but did they have the determination or the desperation that it took to succeed?

"What is it like to be . . . a graduate of the American Academy
and ready for all the great roles ever written?" Robinson would
ask years later in his autobiography. "I'll tell you what it's like:
It's sheer frustration. You are ready for every challenge, and there
are none."

Carnegie, upon graduation, auditioned for a part in one of four
road companies of Molly Mayo's *Polly of the Circus*. To his amazement, the audition concluded with the words that every young,
striving actor most wants to hear: "Young man, you've got the
part!"

Thrilled at the unexpected news, Carnegie settled the bill at
his boarding house and took to the road for forty-two and a half
weeks of one-night stands. He was just one of more than twenty-
seven performers.

Polly of the Circus, starring Mabel Taliaferro and Malcolm Wil-
liams in the original cast, had been one of the hits of the 1907
season, running for 160 performances. It was pure melodrama
that drew crowds for a couple of good reasons. First, it suggested
a rather sensuous liaison between a pure and lovely bareback
rider in the circus (Polly) and a handsome young minister. Second, it offered great spectacle. During the third act, acrobats,
trapeze artists, clowns, musicians, barkers, and other extras all
appear on stage in a full-scale circus performance.

The play opens with the Big Top being put up outside the
local parsonage in a small Ohio town. The first night, Polly the
bareback rider is injured when she jumps through a hoop. Because the local hospital has just burned, the most logical place
to take her is into the house of the young clergyman. Left behind
to recover, Polly does good deeds for the community, including
teaching Sunday school. The parishioners, however, are shocked
that she continues to live in the clergyman's house. Realizing
that she could be the ruin of his career, Polly virtuously bids
him farewell. But eventually the circus returns to town. Unable

to stay away, the young minister goes to the performance. Polly sees him as her horse is rounding the ring. She slips . . . falls . . . and the minister catches her in his arms.

After a change of scene and some dialogue, Polly and the minister embrace and say some tender words. The final scene is a tableau. Engaged to be wed, Polly and her young man stand side by side, watching as the circus wagons pull out of town.

With the help of heavy makeup, a frock coat, and a doctor's kit, Carnegie played the part of kindly Dr. Hartley, who rushes to Polly's assistance when she falls through the hoop. Since parts were doubled by the performers, Carnegie also had to play a clown or barker during the circus scene in act three. More experienced actors played the lead roles.

However little he learned about drama with this company, Carnegie certainly learned about life on the road. The cast usually left town around midnight, after the set had been struck and trundled down to a freight car. Waiting in a dimly lit station, the actors chatted, drowsed, smoked, and warmed their hands by the potbelly stove as they waited for the train to come in. Usually they arrived at the next station well before dawn—when the extras had to help unload the sets from the railroad cars and put them aboard freight wagons to carry to the theater. Only the stars got to sleep in Pullman cars.

The actors earned next to nothing. Many of them had to do double duty as stagehand, stage manager, or prop person. Once in town, they stayed in theatrical boardinghouses recommended by other troupers. It was standard practice to save on laundry by wearing "thousand-mile shirts"—drab-colored shirts that never showed the dirt, even if they weren't laundered. They ate quick meals at cheap lunch counters or subsisted on stale sandwiches, peanuts, and soda pop that were peddled by barkers in the railroad cars. The quickest way to get a new makeup cloth was to filch a towel from alongside the boardinghouse wash basin.

At one point, Carnegie was in the same road company with Howard Lindsay, and they roomed together. Lindsay recalled that Carnegie used to make pocket money by selling suitcases and ties. Every penny helped.

Still, it could have been worse. At least Carnegie had a part. He got to travel and to speak his few lines before a live audience. Plus he had the experience of working with actors and actresses who displayed their feathers: made their demands; fought; sulked; screamed; demanded more attention, more money, or more comforts. But no matter what emotional outbursts occurred, they were all in it together. When one of the company was down and out, the others gave generously. When one was sick, the others filled in. All put heart and soul into their passionate, melodramatic performances.

END OF AN ACTING CAREER

After the tour ended, Carnegie returned to New York. Forsaking his grim cell in the West Forties, he found another furnished room at 244 West 56th Street. Joining the hordes of actors who were "at liberty" (a widely understood euphemism for unemployed), Carnegie began to haunt the offices of agents and producers along Broadway.

Having experienced some ten months of thousand-mile shirts, stale sandwiches, and sleepless nights in the hard-backed, kidney-wrenching seats of railroad cars, Carnegie was not highly motivated to try out for any more touring companies. When he went for parts on Broadway, however, again and again he heard the same reply: "Sorry, nothing for you today."

Perhaps it was the humiliation of being told time and again that he didn't have the necessary skills or experience or maybe it was the bleak prospect of more experiences like *Polly of the Circus* that made Carnegie withdraw from show business. With nearly two years and so many hopes tied up in his dream of becoming an actor, the decision was difficult. In the coming years, as he struggled along with his courses and saw fellow students like Howard Lindsay and Guthrie McClintic rise to fame in the theater world, there were times when he would regret the decision to leave the stage.

In one rueful moment after *How to Win Friends* was published, Carnegie reflected on his decision to end his career on the stage:

> Theodore Dreiser, in his youth, sat in a chair in the outer office of the *Chicago Globe* all day and every day for over a month, until they finally consented to give him a job. How I wish that I had done that in some producer's office! Just think how it might have changed my life!

A ROLE-PLAYING SESSION

In the Carnegie course, a role-playing session occurs on the eleventh night the class meets. The instructor invites one woman to sit on a folding chair near the front of the room. After a demonstration by the instructor, a young man in a dark, well-cut business suit leaps from his chair and crouches in front of the seated woman. He raises his clasped hands in the air and cries: "Daisy Mae, Daisy Mae. I just *looooves* you, Daisy Mae. I could just *squeeeeze* you to death."

At the word "squeeze," he wraps his arms together, squeezing himself as his eyes close in a grimace of pleasure and longing.

The instructor, standing at "Daisy Mae's" side, shakes her head skeptically. "Do you believe him, class?"

The class is laughing. "No!" they roar.

"Let's hear it again!" says the instructor.

And the businessman, still down on his knees, repeats the words from the Carnegie script:

"DAISY MAE, OOOOH, DAISY MAE. I JUST *LOOOOVES* YOU, DAISY MAE. I COULD JUST *SQUEEEEZE* YOU TO DEATH."

"*Now* do you believe him?" asks the instructor.

"Yes!" roars the class.

"Daisy Mae" is just one example of the melodramatic scenarios that are scripted for Dale Carnegie students. During the next hour and a half, everyone in the class will play many different roles in scenes that are, by turn, ridiculous, melodramatic, embarrassing, and hilarious. It's as if every scene of *Polly of the Circus* were being reenacted again and again by hundreds of thousands of Carnegians, decades after Carnegie himself appeared as Dr. Hartley in small towns across America.

The exercise is somewhere between charades and an amateur theatrical performance. For students who have difficulty overcoming inhibitions, the scripted roles and the exaggerated character parts give them permission to play parts that are, by turn, romantic, fearful, and boisterous.

Initially, the role playing is embarrassing for some. But since everyone has to play their part on the small classroom stage, no one person is singled out over anyone else. And the instructor keeps the scenarios moving along at a rapid pace—so embarrassment is quickly dissipated by the applause and laughter that follow each scene.

One can hear Mr. Sargent turning over in his grave. Is this burlesque how Carnegie chooses to honor the AADA's contributions to the annals of American drama? With thousands of charade performances in hundreds of evening classes all across America? Was it for this that Steele MacKaye and the idealistic theorists of twentieth-century American drama dedicated their lives to the theater?

No, Dale Carnegie had another purpose in mind, and so he cannot really be faulted for borrowing role-playing techniques from the AADA and his experience on the road, or for incorporating melodramatic themes from 1910-era Broadway plays. In the Dale Carnegie Course the purpose of role-playing is not to teach better acting, but to loosen up the students and allow them to explore artificiality as well as naturalism. The exercise teaches them to remember lines, *be* ridiculous, break down barriers, and discover that it's all right to overact.

For some students—those who never acted before, who never played any role other than themselves—this is an evening of real self-discovery.

SELF-DISCOVERY

At a recent Dale Carnegie session, Marie, a twenty-three-year-old woman with a sallow complexion and short straight hair stands in front of the class. In an earlier session, she talked in an almost inaudible voice about the long hours she spent at home, taking care of her bedridden father. Now it is her turn to take a role in front of the class. She glances toward the instructor, who has just told Marie what she is supposed to do, and who nods.

Marie hunches her shoulders, points a finger, and makes a sweeping gesture.

"Feeeeeee!" Her voice is muted, eyes downcast. She doesn't look at the class.

"That's it!" urges the instructor in an undertone.

Crouching lower, reaching out farther this time, Marie makes another gesture, and her voice takes on some strength.

"Fiiiiiiiiiiiie!"

There's the glimmer of smile now. She glances at the first row of eyes watching her.

"FOOOOOOOE!" (Her voice is *much* stronger now.) "FUM!" (She smiles!)

She straightens. Sniffs.

"*I* SMELL ... THE ... BLOOD ..."

She sniffs again. Shaking her finger, and in a voice louder than ever before, she goes on:

"OF AN *ENGLISH* ... *MUN!*"

As the short monologue continues, Marie needs no more urging from the instructor. The class is watching her closely.

"BE HE *SHORT* OR BE HE *LEAN* ..."

Marie, playing the giant, scans the crowd, searching for the scrawny Englishman as she sniffs the air. The moment is transcendent. Marie *is* the giant, on the prowl, mean, arrogant, and hungry—a Marie the class has never seen before and perhaps never will again.

Moments later, applause for her performance has ended, the next giant is in front of the class, and Marie is back in her seat again, hands folded, a tinge of color in her cheeks.

Toward the end of class, the instructor makes an analogy with a Slinky toy. "In this class," she explains, holding a Slinky in her hand, "You have been stretched." She expands the wire-coil toy between her hands, then collapses it to its unstretched state and holds it in the palm of one hand. "You are just the same as you were before this class. But you know that you *can* be stretched without losing your shape. That's what we've seen here tonight."

FROM ACTING TO SPEAKING

When Carnegie first started the course, this eleventh session was devoted to enunciation and elocution rather than improvisation and pantomime. The change to the present-day exercise is significant, for it represents the shift from an emphasis on careful speech and clear diction to an emphasis on expressiveness, body movement, and emotional force.

Essentially, when he transformed public-speaking styles in his fourteen-session course, Carnegie paralleled the change in American acting style brought about by Steele MacKaye and his followers at the AADA. Up to the turn of the century, actors learned acting—how to stand, how to speak, how to gesture—according to standards passed on through many generations of classical directors. Although Americanisms were beginning to creep into dramatic dialogue, the King's English was still the language of choice on Broadway. Audiences might be soaking up melodramatic dreck, but it all seemed extremely refined if it sounded like teatime at Windsor Castle.

With MacKaye and others on his side there came a revolution in rhetorical style in the American theater. With Dale Carnegie (and there were others on *his* side as well) there came a rhetorical revolution in public speaking.

The seeds for both revolutions were planted by MacKaye's teacher, a French singing and acting teacher named Francois Delsarte who reacted against the posturing artificiality prized by the Paris Conservatoire. Delsarte strongly believed in the primacy of movement. He taught that action and gesture came first, followed by speech, which "comes only to confirm what is already understood by the auditors."

As Delsarte saw it, every individual has three "states of

being"—normal, concentric, and eccentric. The normal state is the calm state that people are in when they are going about their daily lives. The concentric state occurs when a person begins to look inward and concentrate. The eccentric state impels a person toward expansion or extroversion.

In session eleven, Carnegie took his classes out of the normal state and into the eccentric state. As the present-day instructor put it, what happened to people was like a Slinky being expanded from its normal state of rest to an extended, twisting, mobile eccentric state of expansion.

Like his predecessors at the AADA Carnegie was stimulated by the Delsarte principles introduced by MacKaye. Garff B. Wilson, a professor of speech and dramatic art at the University of California, observed in *A History of American Acting* (Indiana University Press, 1966):

> These leaders rejected the practice of teaching attitudes and gestures or of specifying particular vocal devices for the revelation of emotion. They felt that lifelike creation of expression can only develop from within. Thus they emphasized the cultivation of imagination and sensitivity, and they sought to develop not only the intellectual and physical faculties and functions, but "the powers of personality itself—the inner and deeper natures . . . the temperamental and imaginative, instinctive, and conceptively original powers of feeling."

A doer rather than a theoretician, Carnegie changed the design of the session from elocution to role-playing simply because it worked better in the context of the course. It helped students loosen up, relax, extend themselves. The format of that session encouraged them, as he put it, to "expand their comfort zone," so they could feel comfortable with attitudes of expression and emotion beyond their normal range.

Carnegie understood that this must all take place in the safe, controlled conditions of a group that had been building self-confidence and group confidence over the duration of the previous ten sessions. And he structured the exercises so that people would have a chance to wind down. They could return to their normal state before leaving the room. Within the parameters of that one class, however, they could act as silly, loud, boisterous, truculent, passionate, pleading, and bombastic as they wanted.

Carnegie's experience in the theater may have been a source of regret in later years. It was certainly trying and painful while he was enduring it. But he did not let his theater experience go to waste. He was eventually able to interpret, refine, and incorporate his own education in drama into his public-speaking course. A combination of Delsarte's revolutionary principles, MacKaye's intelligent application of those principles, Sargent's inspirational teaching at the Academy, plus a large dose of 1910 melodrama, session eleven is a telling snapshot of Carnegie's brief hour upon the stage.

CHAPTER 4

DOWN AND OUT
IN MANHATTAN

ONE LOOK AT THE YOUNG SALESMAN AND YOU COULD tell he had come upon hard times. Behind the pinkish-frame glasses, there were deep circles under his eyes. He squinted from headaches or sleepless nights. His complexion was too pale even for a city dweller. The features were slightly pinched, though one warm bowl of soup might have been enough to restore an appearance of health.

His clothes showed fastidious care, but still there were telltale signs of poverty. The collar was fresh, the knot of the bow tie was neatly tied, the suit jacket tightly buttoned. But if you looked closely you might catch a glimpse of the stain between the top two buttons of his single-breasted, gray sack suit. The wrinkles behind the knees looked as if they were pressed out every night—only to appear again, etched in the same places, every morning.

This was the Dale Carnegie of 1912, when he was struggling to eke out a living as a Packard car and truck salesman. Packards were priced at the upper end of the market, and New York customers were among the most demanding in the world. Most customers could tell, after a few minutes of conversation with the young salesman, that he did not know much about machines. Even though he enthusiastically praised the "six-38 engine," "force-feed lubrication," and "L-head configuration," these few selling points represented the sum total of his real knowledge of the Packard. Any request for details left him speechless. Instead of giving information that would appeal to a truck mechanic or buyer, Carnegie was likely to launch into a discourse on the integrity of Misters J. W. and William Doud Packard, the founders of the company. To Carnegie, the men who invented America's top-of-the-line trucks and cars were far more interesting than the machines themselves.

Having given up the life of an actor for the life of a Packard truck salesman, Carnegie at age twenty-four was up against some hard realities. The neighborhood where he was living, 56th Street near Eighth Avenue, bordered a district known as Hell's Kitchen. The tenements in this neighborhood were dingy, soot-blackened brick buildings. They had leaky roofs, rusted plumbing, and dingy hallways infested with rats, mice, and cockroaches. Garbage spilled into the alleyways, and the neighborhood reeked of the slaughterhouses, stables, gas plants, and glue and soap factories nearby.

Coming home at night from a wearying twelve-hour day among gleaming, $4 thousand Packard trucks, Carnegie was greeted by the outstretched hands of hoboes hanging around the oil-drum fires on 56th Street. Wailing, smudge-faced children dashed around the curbs and gutters. In the halls of his tenement building, he was greeted by the smell of boiling cabbage. Making his way to his own apartment, he had to avoid the landlord demanding next month's rent.

Worst of all were the roaches. "I still remember," Carnegie wrote more than thirty years later, "that I had a bunch of neckties hanging on the walls; and when I reached out of a morning to get a fresh necktie, the cockroaches scattered in all directions."

Not only was the neighborhood dingy and sordid, it was dangerous. Gangs like the Hudson Dusters, the Gophers, the Gorillas, and Battle Row Annie's Ladies' Social and Athletic Club were so prevalent, that until 1910 the police from the 22nd Precinct would only venture in threes into the Hell's Kitchen neighborhood. Just about the time Carnegie moved into the neighborhood, a strong-arm squad hired by the New York Central Railroad—whose tracks ran down Eleventh Avenue near the Hudson River—began controlling the gangs in Hell's Kitchen. The squad clubbed, shot, and arrested gangsters.

For Dale Carnegie, dining out during those days first meant shopping at Paddy's Market under the Ninth Avenue El between 35th and 42nd Streets. There he had his choice of roasted chicken or sausage cooked by a street vendor over a charcoal brazier, carrots and potato from the Italian woman with the vegetable cart on the corner, and soda bread from the Irish baker. Under the gas street lights beneath the el, Carnegie gathered his banquet together and headed home to his furnished apartment.

More often, he ate at greasy lunch counters frequented by stockyard and railway workers. He speculated that the kitchens of those restaurants had an even greater number of cockroaches than he found among his ties.

"I came home to my lonely room each night with a sick headache," he would recall, "a headache bred and fed by disappointment, worry, bitterness, and rebellion. I was rebelling because the dreams I had nourished back in my college days had turned into nightmares. . . . I longed for leisure to read, and to write the books I had dreamed of writing."

DREAMS OF WRITING

At various times during his life, the dream of writing great novels would grow to become an obsession. Carnegie had harbored that dream from his teenage years. It was only in 1912, however, as a failed actor and mediocre salesman with a furnished apartment in Hell's Kitchen, that he finally said to himself, "What am I doing? If I want to become a writer, why don't I *write*? Why am I wasting my time selling cars I don't care about for a company that won't pay me well enough to live a decent life?"

Carnegie admired writers like Thomas Hardy and perhaps attempted to emulate the British author's brooding, allusive style. But Carnegie's settings were pure Americana. He wanted to capture the West, the tribulations of life on a Missouri farm, the strength of character of people like his own mother and father, the atmosphere of the cornfield and the general store. He could not have chosen more unsuitable models for his own novels than those of Thomas Hardy. The conflict of intention and execution made it impossible for Carnegie to satisfy himself—or, for that matter, any agent or publisher.

But the role of writer helped Carnegie to live a satisfying vicarious existence. Through his writing he could be a preacher, missionary, and teacher. Writing novels brought back the actor in him, as he leapt into the roles of the characters who peopled his pages. Above all, writing provided him with a legitimate escape, by way of the imagination, from bleak urban reality. Once he took pen in hand, his mind drifted back to the Missouri farmlands.

Writing was an ideal solution to his current dilemma. All it required was pen and paper. Those materials, at least, he could afford. Now, if he could only be published, he would have entree to the fascinating literary world of New York. He imagined hobnobbing with Jack London, Frank Norris, and Henry James. If only he had time to apply his energy to writing, he was certain the world would recognize his talents.

Furthermore, a popular novel could be profitable! Readers of the day were hungry for novels that were full of local color. Among fictional works that had sold over a million copies between 1900 and 1910 were Jack London's *The Call of the Wild*, *The Tale of the Lonesome Pine* by John Fox, Jr., *Rebecca of Sunnybrook Farm* by Kate Douglas Wiggin, and *The Shepherd of the Hills* by Harold Bell. The age of the blockbuster book had dawned.

Carnegie had in mind a novel that would tell the waiting public everything they wanted to hear about the life of a young man growing up in Missouri. He would write about the flirtations, romances, and town gossip, the hardships of tilling the fields and caring for livestock, and the courage and strong faith of brave men and women who persevered against all odds.

Every day, as he made his way home to 244 West 56th Street, Carnegie envisioned a saga of epic proportions. Each scene became abundantly clear in his imagination.

Writing this great Western novel had been the dream conceived in his college days. But how could he recapture that dream when he was scraping together every penny just to make ends meet? He was always so exhausted at the end of a day in the Packard show room that he could scarcely stagger back to his apartment and collapse into bed.

The desperation had begun to tell, in the form of psychosomatic headaches, insomnia, and depression. He decided he had to quit his job. "I knew I had everything to gain and nothing to lose by giving up the job I despised," he later recalled. "I wasn't interested in making a lot of money, but I was interested in making a lot of living."

But giving up his job would be hopeless unless he had something else to do. And what *could* he do? What were the talents and abilities that would enable him to earn a living?

Nothing in his career, so far, had proved quite so rewarding as the public speaking he taught to others at Warrensburg State Teachers College.

Looking at the turns his career had taken, he saw that he had received an unexpected benefit from his short training as an actor. Now he had in his portfolio not only the salesman's experience but also an actor's training. These qualifications, he felt, made him eminently qualified to teach others the art of public speaking.

Why couldn't he be paid to teach others how to speak? Surely there were many businessmen who could learn the skills he had to offer. And if that was the case, why shouldn't he earn his living teaching them at night? By day, he could pursue what he really wanted to do—writing books.

Carnegie quit his job with Packard and applied for a position teaching public speaking in a night extension course at Columbia University. He was turned down. He visited New York University with the same request. Again, his application was rejected.

Desperately seeking an alternative, he heard about the YMCA night schools, which many business people attended. Surely, their standards for instructors would be modest enough. Carnegie knew that, once in the classroom, he could inspire his students. All he needed was a chance.

WAYS OUT OF WORRY

Looking back on various moments in his own life, Carnegie saw cycles of worry, fear, and inertia, interspersed with action, improvement, and recovery. When he recalled the worries he'd had as a young boy, he often reflected that his greatest fears (such as being buried alive) were fruitless and unnecessary. Although his poverty had caused him constant distress, his family had survived. Perhaps he was even the better for it. Similarly, the despair he'd felt when he lost speaking contests at college gave way to triumph when he won all the prizes just a year later. Typically, he seized his bleakest hour, as a down-and-out Packard salesman in New York, to take direct action that would improve his life and help bring him closer to his dreams.

Reflecting on these transitions—especially with the added perspective of more years—Carnegie saw a common theme in his own experiences. Worry and fear were internal forces that held him back. *Conquering* worry and fear gave him a new hold on life.

Did other men and women have this pattern to their lives? He suspected they did, even though they might not admit it. Later, he would use the Dale Carnegie Course as a forum for discussing a topic that would have been taboo in any academic program. Let people talk about their fears and worries. That could become the first step toward conquering them!

In the Dale Carnegie Course, all students are assigned to think about "an incident related to controlling worry and fear." Initial reactions to this assignment frequently range from indifference ("What, me worry?") to fatalism ("I worry all the time—I can't help it.").

Since the assignment is nonspecific, people may speak about any topic. Like most Carnegie assignments, this is one in which people do not look farther than their own experiences for examples. Practically everyone worries about something—a job, a school assignment, children, finances, a deadline, a disaster. People worry about their cars, their neighborhoods, their houses, their image. They worry what people may say about them, and they worry that what they say about others may come *back* to them.

But what do they do to *control* that worry?

In session ten of a recent class, Connie Hill steps to the front of the room. A slim, white-haired woman with brightly painted lips, she is very neatly dressed in a pale blue dress. Facing the class, she holds up a set of codes published by the state. Her gestures are controlled; her expression is pleasant but impassive. She enunciates clearly. Everything about her appearance and demeanor is calm and assured. Holding up the blue-covered booklet so everyone can see, she says:

> Right now, this is the most important document in my life. These are the laws for incarceration of the mentally ill in this state. One clause in this booklet says an adult can be committed only if someone can prove that his conduct endangers the life or safety of another person.

She places the document on a table next to her and lifts her eyes to the class again.

> My son, Tim, is a patient in a state mental hospital. I can't explain why, but he blames me for his condition, and he has threatened my life. This has been a great burden to me.

When my husband was alive, I could share it with him. But now that he's gone, I have to carry this by myself.

I have other children. For many years, I never talked to them about what happened with Tim. I never told them that he was threatening me.

A few years ago, I went into therapy. The therapist convinced me that I should tell my other children what was going on. I couldn't keep the truth from them any longer.

So I did. I told them. My children hate Tim for what he's done to me. They blame him for everything. When I'm with my other children, we don't talk about him very much.

And I don't talk to other people about Tim. I live with this every day. It's with me all the time. I have learned to take each day as it comes.

My point to you is that you can learn to live with worry if you take each day as it comes. The benefit will be that you won't worry about things that you can't change.

The class applauds. Connie picks up the state codes for the incarceration of the insane and returns to her seat.

Later in the class, Jay Kaiser—a stocky, athletic young man with the build of a bantamweight fighter—tells how difficult it was for him to begin classes in night school:

I always worry about my assignments. When I have a paper due, I'll begin worrying two weeks ahead, thinking "What am I going to say? How am I going to get it done?" Last week, I sat down to write a paper and I was so worried, I couldn't even begin writing. So I said to myself, "What is the worst that can happen?" The worst that can happen is I won't be able to do this paper. It's only one-quarter of my grade, so if I don't do it, I might get a C. So why don't I try writing *something* and I might get a C+ or a B−. Once I told myself that, it was easy to start, because I'd already considered the worst that could happen.

John Hupert, the heavyset, graying man who stands up next, is a construction worker in his late forties.

About six months ago, I saw the business begin to go downhill. I thought sure I was going to be laid off. Every time the boss called me in, I thought he was going to tell me to pick up my check and go home. I lost a lot of sleep. But here I am, I haven't been laid off, and maybe I won't be. It won't do any good to worry about it. I just take each day as it comes.

Nan Jacobs is an attractive, thirty-two-year-old executive secretary, housewife, and mother. She comes to classes in jeans and running shoes. As she walks to the front of the room, she nods an acknowledgment to another woman in the class:

The first time I came here, Donna and I drove together. She can tell you how scared I was—I was afraid to get out of the car. I was so terrified of standing up in front of an audience, I thought I wouldn't be able to talk. I thought I would faint. But Donna said to me, "Why would that be so terrible if you didn't have anything to say?" I couldn't think of an answer. What was the *worst* that could happen? So I came to class, and I'm glad I did. I'm still afraid—I'm afraid right now—but I know I can do it.

In the isolation of a tenement room on West 56th Street, Dale Carnegie was all alone with his fears and worries, his disappointed ideals and crushing self-doubts. It was only when he left that tenement for the classes at the 125th Street YMCA that he gained greater perspective over all the doubts that were troubling him.

As he wrote later, "A large majority of my students were businessmen—executives, salesmen, engineers, accountants: a cross section of all the trades and professions—and most of them had problems! There were women in the classes, businesswomen and housewives. They, too, had problems! Clearly, what I needed was a textbook on how to conquer worry—so again I tried to find one."

Years later, when he looked in the card catalogue at the New York Public Library, Carnegie discovered that there were nine

times as many books on the subject WORMS as there were on
WORRY (twenty-two on worry, but 189 on worms).

By asking his students to talk about worry, Carnegie gave permission to people to discuss their emotions. They could reveal
the things that caused them anxiety, uneasiness, discouragement, and fear. Such revelations could only happen late in the
course, after the students had spent time together building trust
and confidence in each other. This was not academic classroom
material, and it didn't really fit with the rest of the course. But
to Carnegie, it was one of the most important speeches that any
student could give.

In the years following 1912, as Carnegie refined and perfected
his sessions, he saw that people typically enhanced their speaking skills in the first third of the course. The process of improvement made people receptive to many other kinds of learning.

Carnegie used that receptivity as the foundation for a program
where developing interpersonal skills and fostering a positive, less-
worried outlook became the bulk of the curriculum. He saw that
class members who felt part of the group were likely to accept the
human-relations portion, even if that hadn't been their intention.

The course is not therapy. For the most part, class members
are not dealing with deep-seated psychological problems. More
than half of students are looking primarily for public-speaking
improvement when they sign up. It takes several weeks for group
feelings to become strong. By session ten—when people are
revealing their worries to each other—the class usually feels
quite close. That closeness allows them to reveal the kinds of
feelings that might be revealed in therapy and to do it on assignment. Building on that trust, they grow in many different
respects, taking them far beyond the objectives that they origi-
nally set for themselves.

By the end of the course, only a small percentage of graduates
say that their *primary* gain was acquiring new speaking skills.
Many say that *learning to control worry* was an unexpected
benefit they had never anticipated.

What Carnegie saw in his classes would eventually lead him
to write and publish, in 1948, *How to Stop Worrying and Start
Living*. The book begins with a brief recital of his own traumatic

experience with worry when he was living on the edge of Hell's Kitchen in New York. Finding escape from that worry was a significant turning point in his own life. He hoped that others, too, could use his course and book to overcome worry and act to change their lives.

If Carnegie were alive today, he would be surprised to discover that of all the books listed since 1972 in the New York Public Library, only two fall under the category WORRY.

Does this mean we have turned into a society of nonworriers?

Obviously not. It's just that worry has undergone a change in terminology: there are now 221 titles listed under STRESS.

Hans Selye, a Montreal physician-researcher, started focusing on stress in the 1940s, when Dale Carnegie's course had been in existence for twenty-eight years. Many of the ways of handling stress described by Selye and repeated in numerous self-help books are similar to those discovered by Carnegie.

Essentially, there are two possible courses of action. One, you can do something about the problem or situation that is causing you worry. Two, you can change your attitude toward the problem. Of the thirty rules Carnegie offers in *How to Stop Worrying* as techniques to stop worrying, twenty-one are attitude-related. Basically, these boil down to two concepts—"Don't cry over spilt milk," and "Live in day-tight compartments."

If you want to *do* something about the problem, Carnegie advocated a technique that he picked up from a successful insurance salesman named Frank Bettger, who later toured with Carnegie and wrote his own book on selling. Bettger's technique was to ask himself three questions: What is the problem? What are the possible solutions? What is the answer?

How to Stop Worrying supports the thirty principles with what *The New York Times* book reviewer called "a Bartlett-full quota of sayings." How does the book hold up now? What was common sense in 1948 is still common sense today. The key difference is that the physical consequences of worry were not as well understood then. "Type A" personalities had not been identified as such in 1948, and Carnegie did not have any research statistics relating stress to health.

Because Carnegie focused on the negative aspects of worry,

he didn't mention the positive results that stress can generate. As Hans Selye was to observe, caustically but accurately, "Complete freedom from stress is death."

No one was a greater worrier than Dale Carnegie himself. He tried to apply a good deal of his own medicine to overcome the insomnia, sick headaches, and anxiety about tomorrow's problems that he experienced during the grim days in his New York tenement apartment and at other stressful moments throughout his life. But for him, as for many of his students, a key part of controlling worry was to recognize what was causing the worry.

The process of reading *How to Stop Worrying* and of making a commitment to control worry makes most people realize that they do in fact have concerns that are distracting them. The aging parent who isn't quite able to manage on his own; the hoped-for promotion that hasn't yet come through; the twelve-year-old son who's getting poor grades—any of these concerns can be candidates for full-scale worries.

Carnegie's thirty principles provide an array of remedies, all of which may be worth a try. Each person taking the Carnegie course tries to apply those principles and report on what happens. Then the power of the group takes over. Listening to stories of how Carnegie's principles worked for others reinforces the desire to keep applying those commonsense guides.

There is a recurring theme in these stories. People who have focused on changing their attitudes have discovered that, as worry lifted, they increased their ability to deal with the problem causing the worry in the first place. As Carnegie found out, when you begin dealing with worry, you may become better at setting goals and acting.

In 1912, in his apartment on 56th Street, Carnegie learned to get through the day by living one day at a time. The experience was grim, but like the other experiences in his life, he learned from it and drew a lesson from it. It was fortunate that he confronted his problems by chasing away the cockroaches, finding a necktie, and heading north for his interview at the 125th Street YMCA. Fortunate, because he was taking a step that would help millions of other people control and conquer worry.

CHAPTER 5

AN ACCIDENTAL BEGINNING

T HE YMCA THAT OVERLOOKED THE BROAD EXPANSE of 125th Street of Harlem in 1912 was a stately five-story building. Stores and apartment buildings flanked it. With a stepped facade leading up to an ornate gable in which the letters YMCA were inscribed in stone, it was dignified and imposing.

Despite the dignity of the structure, the advertising on the front and side clearly marked this as more of a community center than the type of private men's club one might find downtown. Bold letters on the side of the upper stories announced: Gymnasium–Swimming Pool–Evening School. A painting illustrated a genteelly suited gentleman diving headfirst toward the *n* in "Gymnasium."

In front, a placard advertised, "Harlem Evening School—Prepare Now for a Better Job," and "5 W. 125th St. Gymnasium—Best of Good Fellowship." Although by 1930, this part of Harlem would be an all-black neighborhood, in 1912 its population was still predominantly white and heavily Jewish. The 125th Street YMCA was for whites only; the Colored Men's YMCA was still down on West 53rd Street.

The YMCA was in no way the educational equivalent of Columbia and NYU, which had already turned Carnegie down. Nonetheless, it could be a major opportunity for him. He could teach at night and write during the day. Surely with his debate training plus his sales and acting experience, he'd get a chance to help young businessmen "prepare now for a better job."

As it turned out, the director of the 125th Street Y did give him a chance. He told Carnegie he could audition at a social evening. Reaching back to the skills he developed at Warrensburg State, Carnegie recited a poem by James Whitcomb Riley, the "Hoosier Poet." The verses of "Knee Deep in June" recalled his Missouri farm days:

Tell you what I like the best
'Long about knee-deep in June
'Bout the time the Strawberries melts
On the vine—some afternoon
Like to jes' get out and rest,
And not work at nothin' else!

Orchard's where I'd ruther be—
Needn't fence it in fer me!—
Jes' the whole sky overhead, And the whole earth
    underneath—
Sort o' so's a man kin breathe
Like he ort, and kind o' has
Elbow room to keerlessly
Sprawl out len'thways on the grass
Where the shadders thick and soft
As the kivvers on the bed

Mother fixes in the loft
Allus, when they's company!

The oration was met with applause. Success! Now he had to strike a deal with the director. Carnegie requested the usual salary for night-school teachers: $2 per session. The director looked skeptical. The Y had never before tried a public-speaking course. He doubted it would draw enough students to warrant such a salary. He reminded Carnegie that the Y would bear the expenses. "So I said," Carnegie remembered, " 'I will work on a profit-sharing basis.' "

The prospect was unsettling. The whole idea of a night job was to generate a steady income that would free days for writing. But Carnegie had nowhere else to turn. He had set a goal of teaching public speaking. If there was any place in the city to teach, it would be here.

A few minutes into his first class he hit trouble. He looked out at a collection of blank faces and panicked. He didn't know what to say. The tutoring techniques that had worked well with his classmates at Warrensburg weren't working with these businessmen. Learning how to emulate Edmund Burke wouldn't help them get ahead in business. Nor would teaching a repertoire of hand gestures earn Carnegie the income he wanted. His students wanted results—the poise to stand on their feet and give an effective presentation; the ability to participate effectively in meetings. How could he inspire his students? How could he wake them up?

With a sudden inspiration that determined the course of the rest of his life, Carnegie asked a man in the back row to stand up. "Give us a brief impromptu talk," Carnegie told him.

"Talk? What can I talk about?" responded the man.

"Talk about yourself. Tell us something about your background, your life."

Carnegie's idea to get people talking worked. In three seasons he was earning $30 a night in commissions compared to the $2 a night salary the YMCA had refused to pay. And the idea remains the foundation of the course today. The key was getting class members on their feet to talk about topics they knew. Carnegie prodded them: What makes you angry? Tell us about something exciting that happened when you were a child. Think of an experience that taught you a lesson.

EVENINGS AT THE Y

Not by accident did Dale Carnegie start his course in a YMCA. Back in 1912, YMCAs, YWCAs, and YMHAs were important educational organizations. Along with the Boy Scouts, Girl Scouts, Campfire Girls, and fraternal groups such as Rotary, Kiwanis, and Lions, they were the major organizations concerned with the education of adults.

Adult education was booming by 1912 in the United States. The American Lyceum, founded in 1831, had been first. Its principal purpose was to foster public schools, and a few years after its founding, there were 3,000 town lyceums. The American Lyceum accomplished much and then faded, but fostered such successors as the Chautauqua program.

Correspondence study had sprung up after the Civil War. The International Correspondence Schools of Scranton, Pennsylvania, source of the courses peddled by Dale Carnegie during his first days as a salesman, was founded in 1891. It grew to be the largest and best known profit-oriented correspondence school in the world. Universities entered the extension field in the early 1890s, but following a short period of rapid growth, they experienced a fifteen-year period of decline.

The years from 1910 to 1919, however, when Carnegie was establishing his public-speaking course in New York and Philadelphia, were expansion years for university extension as well. And the period from 1920 to World War II encompassed growth years for both Carnegie and university extension for similar reasons. Young men looking for jobs were moving to the cities. An increasing number of jobs required high levels of skills. The prime motivation for the evening college student was the acquisition of some special knowledge that would help in getting ahead. This desire is still the key motivator for adults in either nonprofit or proprietary adult-education programs.

When he struck a deal with the YMCA to take a portion of the receipts rather than a flat teaching fee, Carnegie made an important discovery about himself. He didn't have to sell a *product* to be a salesman. He could make a significant commission by selling his skills and ability. And as long as he effectively sold his skills, class by class, night after night, he would indeed achieve his original goal. He would have the time to write, if his teaching gained results.

LEARN BY DOING

That first evening in 1912, Carnegie was beginning to discover the key elements in teaching public speaking to adults. Those first classes taught him an important lesson about teaching the businessman who found his way into his classroom. Among Carnegie's discoveries:

- Fear is the basic cause of ineffective speaking. A young man, self-assured seated across a desk from a prospect, could become incoherent when asked to make a presentation on his feet. Carnegie's challenge was to make that young man feel comfortable as soon as possible.
- Many flaws are the result of speaking on a topic a speaker has no feeling for or knowledge of. Only remedying the preparation would remedy these flaws. Too often students took on subjects over their heads. Carnegie discovered the best assignment was a simple one. Talk about a childhood experience; share something that makes you angry. Don't stretch for supposed worthy, important topics.
- Positive reinforcement and the absence of negative criticism in the first few sessions are the most effective way to build confidence and, consequently, speaking effectiveness. Most of these young men were criticized daily by their bosses and put down by their customers. Most had gone through a school

system that punished them when they stepped out of line. No wonder they were afraid to speak up! They needed rewards and encouragement, not more criticism. By coincidence, the building where Carnegie started teaching was just a few blocks from Columbia University. There John Dewey was simultaneously developing an educational philosophy that had the same bias for action. If knowledge involves doing, Dewey argued, then genuine learning can be achieved only by doing. Carnegie, who had no intellectual or philosophical foundation for his curriculum, developed a course where no one could sit passively for the session. At least once a session, and usually twice, a class member had to get out of his seat and talk to the entire group.

In similar practical fashion, Carnegie created a friendly, supportive environment for learning. He filled the classroom with mutual respect and trust. He also made class fun. If he didn't make the four-hour evening sessions exciting, his students would have been bored after a full day's work. It was more effective to let the students do more speaking than the instructor. This approach also made it less wearying for Carnegie to teach night after night.

That Carnegie succeeded as an independent instructor at the YMCA when he couldn't even get his foot in the door at Columbia or NYU was probably the best possible thing that could have happened to him. It certainly did alter the destiny of the Dale Carnegie program. It meant that he would be forever free to experience, improvise, discard, and implement new methods with a total disregard for all principles save two:

- Did it work with his students?
- Did it keep them coming back for more?

As an independent instructor, he had to keep them coming back because they did not have any outside requirements to fulfill beyond their own self-motivation. As the Dale Carnegie organization has quietly grown to a business with annual revenues exceeding $100 million, it has shunned the educational establishment. It likes to view itself as practical, as opposed to theoretical—an educational business that has to prove itself every day or enrollments will dry up.

Proprietary and nonprofit educational enterprises have always had an "us versus them" relationship. In the three-quarters of a century since Dale Carnegie created his public-speaking course, the Dale Carnegie course and organization have moved from being on the cutting edge of adult education to sitting right in the mainstream. By 1938, a professor of speech could tell his colleagues at the twenty-third annual convention of the National Association of Teachers of Speech:

> The best public speaking in America today—and the best teaching—is found in the classes of the Dale Carnegie Institute. And the reason is this—they concentrate on teaching public speaking.

THE EVOLUTION

How did a one-man program, begun in a YMCA classroom in 1912, grow into the international network of instructors and programs that exists today? Remarkably, the guiding principles have remained much the same. Modest changes in teaching methods, instructional materials, and program design have resulted from evolution and necessity.

Evolution occurred because Carnegie was a perfectionist. He always saw ways to improve. Necessity was a matter of survival. The entire Dale Carnegie course and institution has always been an independently financed and self-promoting organization. It has always been outside the boundaries of any publicly funded educational institution. That was one of its sustaining qualities. Since it was independent and under the control of one guiding individual for its first forty-two years, innovation and experimentation were always possible.

As the course evolved, Dale Carnegie began to realize it was no longer primarily a course in public speaking. The course led directly to confidence building and increased personal effectiveness. From a marketing perspective, however, it has always been sold in large measure as an effective speaking course.

Carnegie's methods of marketing the public speaking course went through a transition at the end of World War II. In the prewar days, responsibility for selling the course rested largely on the shoulders of its founder. Although a number of for-profit business schools around the country offered the course before the war, Carnegie was doing most of the teaching himself. Since he was competing with many nonprofit adult-education programs, Carnegie had to sell the course to prospective students. And to do that, he had to convince his prospects that the value of his course more than offset the cost of enrolling.

The immense success of Carnegie's book, *How to Win Friends and Influence People*, changed the equation by generating a great deal of outside interest in the course. No longer did Carnegie have to concentrate on selling. Now it was a matter of keeping up with demand. People were coming to him and asking where they could take the course. In 1944 Carnegie switched to the licensing system that operates today in order to meet this demand.

Dale Carnegie & Associates licenses territories to sponsors who pay a percentage of revenues. Sponsors agree to follow the instructional guidelines set forth by the home office. Unlike licensees in most businesses, however, the sponsor does not own the rights to the course in his territory. After the sponsor retires, the rights revert to Dale Carnegie & Associates, which then chooses another sponsor.

Not all territories are licensed operations. In sixteen cities, including New York, Washington, and Houston, the operations are company owned. A sponsorship can be quite lucrative. Ralph Nichols, for instance, is the highly successful sponsor in the Detroit area. He made the cover of *U.S. News & World Report* as an example of an ordinary individual who became a millionaire.

Today, more than 3 million men and women are Carnegie graduates. Another 165,000 or so take the training each year. Despite its size, which makes it one of the world's largest adult-education operations, very few teachers of speech have adopted any of the Carnegie methods. In the nineteen twenties and thirties a number of academics had become curious about the teaching methods the Carnegie course used to get results in speaking and personal development.

William Millson, a university speech professor, warned in 1941 that teachers of speech should familiarize themselves with Carnegie methods. They should "test by trial any that are new before rejecting them through prejudice against commercialization, which we can all condemn."

He recommended adopting some of the Carnegie methods. More than touting a particular teaching method, Millson valued the emotional and social side of the Carnegie course. He admired its lack of emphasis on the practical and technical aspects of speech skills. In spite of this early interest, the gap between the commercial Carnegie course and academic speech departments has been almost unbridgeable.

Occasionally, someone who takes the course becomes filled with enthusiasm for what it accomplishes and starts to sing its praises. In the 1950s, for example, a psychiatrist named David Fink wrote a popular book called *Be Your Own Self*. He advised teachers of *all* subjects to take the Dale Carnegie Course to experience its teaching methods. "The methods used in teaching this course today," he said, "will become the methods of teaching all courses tomorrow."

Also in the 1950s, the first attempt was made to bridge the gulf that had existed between Carnegie and academia since the start of the course. Paul Brownstone, a speech teacher from Penn State, wrote a dissertation comparing the Dale Carnegie Course to similar adult-education courses at Brooklyn College.

Both courses, he concluded, were well run and delivered what they promised. He felt Carnegie had superior instructors and provided better materials. The big difference was cost. The fee for the Carnegie course was $134, versus $10 at Brooklyn College. Instructors were also paid differently. A Carnegie instructor earned $30 for a two-and-a-half-hour session. At Brooklyn College the compensation ranged from $5 to $10 per hour. Today there remains a big difference in fees. The current charge for the Dale

Carnegie course is as much as $900. At Brooklyn College the fee for a public-speaking course is now $110; at New York University, the fee is $240.

MANAGEMENT EDUCATION

In 1912, management education was an unknown concept. Adult education was in full swing, stimulated by urbanization. It was not, of course, the multibillion dollar business that it is today.

As adult education increasingly becomes a subject of study in its own right, a number of its distinctive characteristics are being identified. More adult programs are being designed around principles very different from traditional education. The Dale Carnegie Course has long used many of these same techniques, largely because it developed on its own and was meant for adults from the beginning.

Adults typically want to enhance or develop a skill that will increase their effectiveness in some area of life. Typically, a life-cycle event—marriage, professional change, moving, the death of a friend or relative—triggers the readiness to learn.

The median age of a Carnegie course student has long been the mid-thirties. According to the concept of developmental stages, the key tasks in one's late twenties and early to mid-thirties are settling into an occupation and defining family relationships. Not surprisingly, these developmental tasks lead to related educational activities. With its combination of personal and professional skill enhancement, the Carnegie course touches the main concerns of its target audience.

Almost from the very beginning, Dale Carnegie realized that only a few of his students would have frequent opportunities to use their newfound speaking skills. Getting along with people at work, being a better husband and father, worrying less, having a positive attitude to set a continuing series of goals—these were skills that a graduate could use every day.

From his first night of teaching, Carnegie was market-driven. He wasn't interested in educational theory, departmental authority, or academic legitimacy. He wanted satisfied students, so he gave them what worked. He wanted referrals, so he looked for ways to address more aspects of his students' lives. When he saw a need for enhancing interpersonal skills, he incorporated that into the course. He did the same when he incorporated the control of worry into the course.

Recently, educators have concluded that motivation in adult education is based less on external rewards such as a better job or a salary increase than on internal factors such as self-esteem and self-actualization. This was the discovery that Carnegie began to make when he first asked his students to talk about something they knew. Whether it was a description of a bus ride, the rescue of a brother from drowning, or an awkward sales call, speakers gained confidence when they talked about what they knew, rather than what they thought they should know.

Not public-speaking skills, not interpersonal skills, but self-confidence—that's what Dale Carnegie would eventually decide his course was all about. Now, more than thirty years after his death, it remains the foundation for the fourteen sessions. It also is the one skill or concept that you cannot develop through studying *How to Win Friends* or *The Quick and Easy Way to Effective Speaking*. Thus it is an underlying reason the course thrives.

SELF-CONFIDENCE

But what is self-confidence? To Dale Carnegie, it was the poise and self-assurance that he saw thousands of nervous, awkward speakers develop as they grew comfortable being on their feet in front of a group.

An incident that occurred in an early session illustrates the point. Carnegie had induced one nervous class member to stand up and begin speaking, but the man was so overcome with fear that he fainted. Carnegie salvaged the moment. He stood beside the fallen speaker and proclaimed that he would deliver a successful talk in a month. And the student did.

In his classes, Carnegie saw people grow to meet each other

with firmer handshakes. They held their heads higher. The nervous pacer learned to stand in one spot. The uncertain voice began projecting to the back of the room. The stiff arms started to gesture naturally. Downcast eyes began to make contact with everyone in the room. Naturally, Carnegie wasn't the only one to perceive these changes. Even as a student sat through a class fretting about his or her performance, that person couldn't help but notice the changes in the other people in the room. Gradually, it dawned that these same changes might be happening in himself or herself as well.

The newfound confidence went beyond being in front of an audience. As the course developed, Carnegie increasingly sent class members out into the world to test their confidence in real-life situations. He enjoyed seeing someone develop poise in front of a group, but was there a carryover into the rest of life? And if there was, what exactly was happening?

FOUNDATIONS IN EXPERIENCE

Carnegie depended on the varied and rich experiences of his students to make the classroom experience work. Carnegie knew the course could never be a lecture program. In the early days, he often gave lengthy talks, but they were only sales talks or adjuncts to the course itself. Today, the instructor speaks a small fraction of the amount the students do. This fact makes it easier to find and train new instructors; they don't have to be as eloquent as Dale Carnegie was. It is also a convenient way to tap the experience that educators now are realizing adults bring to the classroom.

PACKING THEM IN

In the 1930s, Dale Carnegie was famous for renting hotel ballrooms and holding demonstration meetings. Thousands of prospects would come to hear him and to hear class graduates give testimonials to the course. Usually, a small percentage of attendees would sign up for the course.

In 1937, Carnegie addressed a mass meeting at the Hotel Astor. In words that could be used today to introduce the course, he captured the essence of how it works and how he felt about it.

How do we conquer fear? Well, there's only one way in the world you can permanently conquer fear. There's another way that you can temporarily conquer it—something you get out of a bottle! The only way in the world that I know is to do what Emerson said, "Do the thing that you fear to do and the death of fear is absolutely certain."

So that's the method we use here. We organize these classes. They meet once a week. They have a dinner session from six o'clock to seven forty-five in the evening and an afterdinner session from eight to ten-thirty. Every mother's son and every mother's daughter has to stand up and make a talk—once between six and seven forty-five, and again between eight and ten-thirty in the evening. They have to do that every week—and finally what happens? They begin to see that after all this thing isn't so difficult! They begin to get the hang of it and they begin to get self-confidence. After all, why shouldn't they—and why shouldn't you?

... I know a number of you are saying: "I never could stand up and make a talk!" That's what they all say, but this is what happens. We give away three pencils at each session as prizes.... It doesn't matter how poor a speaker you are to begin with—as a matter of fact, the poorer you are to begin with, the more quickly you are going to begin to get ballots for the red pencil, the first prize for most improvement. That's going to begin to give you a little confidence. And I have discovered this: that no matter how poor a person is, he always finds somebody else in the class of whom he thinks, "Well, I'm a little better than that person!" I'm glad that happens because it gives them confidence and gives them courage....

Some night, some grand, never-to-be-forgotten night, you

are going to carry this pencil home; you're going to wake up your wife, shake it under her nose and say: "Read that! Read that and have a little more respect for me!" And the funny part of it is that she *will* have more respect for you! But what is infinitely more important than that—you are going to have more respect for yourself.

Awards still have much symbolic value and often mark a turning point in a class member's self-perception. But instead of large demonstration meetings, today the organization relies on one-on-one selling. The promotion starts in the classroom.

By a show of hands, how many of you heard about the Dale Carnegie course from a friend? Good. I see almost everybody has his hand up. That's typical, because, nationally, over two-thirds of Dale Carnegie enrollments come from word of mouth.

The scene above is a Dale Carnegie classroom during session nine. A sales representative from the local sponsor is visiting the class. He's asking class members to fill out Opportunity Cards with the names of friends, relatives, or colleagues who might have an interest in the course. These individuals are then contacted, and the sales representative starts the process of persuading that individual—or, more typically these days, that individual's company—to invest in the course.

THE MAGIC OF ENTHUSIASM

Carnegie's inspiration to get his YMCA class of businessmen on their feet and actively participating was ingenious. Not only did it give them a chance to learn by doing, but when coupled with Carnegie's energetic teaching style, it created a classroom full of excitement and enthusiasm.

Carnegie expressed himself not only through the course, but

with a style of instruction that continues to live through its exponents today. The instructor of a Carnegie course moves purposefully to the front of the room. He or she draws people in with a warm, welcoming style. Nothing is studied or learned by rote and, of course, there are no notes.

For three and a half hours the instructor's role is to demonstrate an unflaggingly high energy level. Through comments, demonstrations, and coaching, the instructor works to transmit his or her enthusiasm and excitement to the class.

Unbridled enthusiasm has long been the most off-putting aspect of the Dale Carnegie Course to many people, even while it is one of the course's driving forces. The apparent conflict has never been resolved. Today, the course guide and the printed handout on enthusiasm downplay the external manifestations of enthusiasm in favor of a quietly expressed fervor. Yet the course itself revolves around the very vocal, cheerleader style that Carnegie himself tried to argue wasn't what he meant by enthusiasm.

From the beginning of his course, Carnegie saw that enthusiasm was going to be the key to success. Throughout his writings and speeches, there were numerous attempts to define that elusive quality:

> Now, what is enthusiasm? I hesitate to talk on this subject because in spite of everything I can possibly say, somebody is going to go out thinking that yelling and screaming and pounding the table and carrying on like that is enthusiasm. Well, that's ridiculous. That has nothing whatever to do with enthusiasm.
>
> . . . It's not lung power; it's spirit. It comes from the inside out. Here are some of the synonyms: ardent, eager, exalted, exciting, glowing, heartfelt, inspiring, intense, stimulating, spirited. Now, you don't find anything about noise in there, do you? Or pounding the table or pulling your hair?

There may not have been any noise in the definition, but there was, and continues to be, plenty of noise and table pounding in the course itself. Today, these effusions are integral to certain parts of the course. Although some class members are turned off, the external manifestation of enthusiasm does generate spirit and excitement.

One of the earliest testimonials to Carnegie's enthusiasm was given by a former professional baseball player named Frank Bettger. In 1917, Bettger considered himself a failure. He had been modestly successful in baseball, but had left the sport because of an injury. Now he was about to give up on a fledgling insurance career. As a last-ditch move, he signed up for Dale Carnegie's public-speaking course at a Philadelphia YMCA.

In his own best-selling book *How I Raised Myself from Failure to Success in Selling*, Bettger relates the experience that changed his life.

> One night, Mr. Carnegie stopped me in the middle of a talk. "Mr. Bettger," he said. "Just a moment ... just a moment. Are you interested in what you are saying?"
>
> "Yes ... of course I am," I replied.
>
> Well, then," said Mr. Carnegie, "why don't you talk with a little enthusiasm? How do you expect your audience to be interested if you don't put some life and animation into what you say?"
>
> Dale Carnegie then gave our class a stirring talk on the power of enthusiasm. He got so excited during his talk, he threw a chair up against the wall and broke off one of its legs.

Inspired by Carnegie, Bettger decided to stay in the insurance game. He would put into selling the same enthusiasm that he had put into baseball. "The Magic of Enthusiasm began to work for me in business," he wrote, "just as it had in baseball." Bettger found that he could psych himself up to make cold calls and that—echoing Carnegie—"When I force myself to *act* enthusiastic, I soon *feel* enthusiastic."

The experience of enthusiasm that changed Bettger's life is representative of what other young businessmen were experiencing night after night in Carnegie's courses. Carnegie's pragmatic application of enthusiasm had a firm foundation in the teachings of philosopher and psychologist William James, whom he often quoted:

> Action seems to follow feeling, but really action and feeling go together; and by regulating the action, which is under the more direct control of the will, we can indirectly regulate the feeling, which is not. Hence, act enthusiastic and you'll be enthusiastic.

And when Carnegie saw the idea work for thousands of graduates, he became a firm believer in it. "Act enthusiastic and you'll be enthusiastic" has become a rallying cry used as part of a loud and rambunctious group pep talk. Although enthusiasm can be almost overpowering when everyone in a class is simultaneously shouting out the phrase, that spirit does carry beyond the classroom as well.

While Carnegie himself could change a man's life by breaking a chair in a classroom, in the outside world he would revert to being a paragon of restraint. A mild-appearing, mild-acting figure in a gray business suit, he was notable mostly for his warm and cheery smile. He could wax enthusiastic over a topic. He also was sometimes intensely argumentative, a trait he tried to keep in check. But there is no indication that Carnegie, a lifetime teetotaler and occasional recluse, ever indulged in excesses that would stir comment or controversy. Dale Carnegie in class was Dale Carnegie on stage. Once he left the classroom, he stepped down from the part.

CONVERTS TO ENTHUSIASM

Yet Carnegie observed a change in class members who exaggerated their enthusiasm in class. The exaggeration made converts even of skeptics. Craig Peters, a successful New York lawyer in his mid-thirties, is a recent example of such a skeptic. Peters came to the course to work on his human-relations skills. When it came time in the third session for a group pep talk, he admitted later, he wasn't sure if he was in the right program.

He went through the motions, however. The instructor told the class they were going to get ready by giving themselves a pep talk just the way an athlete will often give himself a pep talk before an important contest. Peters stood with the rest and followed the instructions to "think of three reasons why you're going to give the kind of talk you want to give."

When it came time to shout out with the rest of the class "I'm going to give a good talk because ..." followed by the three reasons he had come up with, Peters just mouthed the words. Ten weeks later, however, after nine more pep talks and a whole session on enthusiasm, he described a conversion. While waiting for a job interview, he gave himself a silent pep talk. He came up with three reasons why he was going to have a successful interview. He did—and he got the job.

The ability of Dale Carnegie to spread the gospel of the magic of enthusiasm has caused it to spread into many organizations. Amway, for example, is a company that thrives on outward displays of enthusiasm that are more typical of Japanese than American companies. Jay Van Andel and Rich DeVos, the cofounders and principals of Amway, are both Dale Carnegie graduates. They have made public and private displays of enthusiasm an integral part of the way they motivate their thousands of distributors. They hold mass rallies that compare to college football rallies and religious revival meetings in the level of enthusiastic outpourings.

Van Andel and DeVos run their company on a series of principles similar to Carnegie's "act enthusiastic and you'll be enthusiastic." Among the principles they promote:

Action conquers fear.

Never accept excuses from yourself.

Believe you can succeed and you will.

Set daily and monthly goals, write them down, and program your subconscious to attain them by surrounding yourself with images of them.

Persistence wins where talent only watches.

Happiness is found only in doing.

Like Dale Carnegie, Van Andel and DeVos have found that enthusiasm often leads people to accomplish more.

In Search of Excellence, the 1980s counterpart to the 1930s *How to Win Friends*, can be read as saying that the cultures of excellent companies foster enthusiasm among employees— whether it's Monday night rallies for people who sell Tupperware, beer busts at Hewlett-Packard, or the sing-alongs at IBM sales training programs.

Leading companies have their own strategies for generating enthusiasm. They range from sales-meeting pep rallies to one-on-one setting of objectives. Many Fortune 500 companies sponsor their employees in Dale Carnegie courses, and a few make attendance almost obligatory for advancement.

John Emery, the longtime head of Emery Air Freight, one of the world's largest airfreight companies, took the course in 1948. He not only continues to send Emery employees to the course, but has developed a management style based on enthusiasm. Emery says:

> Dale Carnegie taught me the power of enthusiasm, and if you can be enthusiastic about what you're doing, no matter what it is, whether you're selling a product, selling a service, or selling yourself, that enthusiasm is contagious, and that's really what part of my job here at Emery is—I'm the head cheerleader.

The head of Domino's Pizza, Tom Monaghan, took the course only a few years ago, well after his firm was on the way to becoming the nation's largest pizza chain. Today, he works very hard to inculcate enthusiasm throughout his organization. The delivery man who races to his car to meet the company's thirty-minute delivery promise is not only promoting his product. He's also working by the Carnegie principle "Be enthusiastic."

Today Dale Carnegie doesn't seem so much a lone voice claiming that enthusiasm is the key to success. Increasingly, American executives are responding to the competitive pressures of the Japanese, whose companies have institutionalized displays of enthusiasm. But Carnegie also realized that in the end you have to *believe* in what you're acting enthusiastic about. A pep talk can get you to work early, and controlled enthusiasm can convince a potential employer that you're the right person for a job. Unless there's genuine feeling, however, you're likely to disappoint yourself and your employer.

Carnegie was fortunate, the day he began his classes at the YMCA. He discovered a career in which he could not only express his enthusiasm, but also arouse that enthusiasm in others. For him, the course in public speaking was the right profession at last. He was combining his education with his experience as salesperson, actor, and teacher, and with his missionary and ministering impulses.

Even his writing would eventually benefit from this self-discovery. His books expressed not only the personal pride that he felt in his own achievements, but also the energy to communicate that feeling of success to others. In one evening back in 1912 in the YMCA, life had finally begun to fall into place for twenty-four-year-old Dale Carnegie.

CHAPTER 6

THE BUSINESS
OF BUSINESS

Ⅰ N 1912, INDUSTRIALIZATION, URBANIZATION, AND IM-
migration were the three forces molding
American business. Since 1865, the population had nearly
tripled, and real per capita income had more than doubled.

Although Dale Carnegie had come east when millions were
heeding Horace Greeley's call to go west, he was part of a national
urbanization that reached a zenith in New York City. In 1880,
only 28 percent of the national population was urban; forty years
later the figure had reached 51 percent.

In 1912, *The New York Times* could boast in an editorial that
in the preceding decade New York and its suburbs had increased in population almost 2 million—"a number so great

that there is no precedent for such an addition to any city anywhere at any time." Growth would have been even larger, the *Times* went on, if the city had not been so disrupted by subway construction: "Just watch New York grow when the subways get going."

A building that was almost complete when Carnegie moved to New York symbolized the changes in the American economy. At 800 feet, the F. W. Woolworth Building had an impressive Gothic splendor. It was the tallest building in the world from 1913 until 1930. Production had become mass production, and distribution had become mass distribution, which Woolworth epitomized.

Woolworth was not the only chain store that was changing the look of American business. There were 200 A&P stores in 1900, 400 in 1912, and 11,000 in 1924. Consumer-oriented magazines such as the *Ladies' Home Journal* and the *Saturday Evening Post* were expanding to serve as guides to the new, good life.

The railroads, more than any other factor, had created the immense national markets for manufacturers and retailers. The automobile, however, was already rivaling the railroad as a mode of transportation. The first Model T appeared in 1908 and cost $845. Henry Ford's constant refinement of production and distribution techniques soon led to lower prices and higher sales. In 1924, the cost was only $290. By 1920, over 8 million cars were registered in America.

As manufacturing and distribution rapidly changed, so did the role of the American businessman. In 1912, the lawyer and later Supreme Court justice, Louis Brandeis, gave a commencement address at Brown University. There he broached the idea that business was becoming a profession. The rise of the railroads and the telegraph had created big business. No longer were virtually all top executives also the owners of the enterprises they managed. And as businesses grew into multiunit enterprises, a new occupation came into existence: the middle manager.

This growth meant that new techniques of management organization and control were needed. Departments were organized; lines of authority, responsibility, and communication were developed; distinctions were made between line and staff functions; and accounting was standardized. These techniques and principles spread from the railroads to other areas of business where operations were becoming more complex.

Educators, albeit slowly at first, became involved in teaching commercial subjects. By 1893, the U.S. Bureau of Education counted 15,220 students enrolled in commercial courses given in public high school and 115,748 enrolled in private commercial or business schools. By 1910, the public schools were catching up. There were 81,249 students in commercial education in public high schools compared to 134,778 in the commercial or business schools. The curriculum in commercial courses consisted of mathematics, writing, business, English, and civics.

There was very little activity in the nineteenth century at the college level in either business or management courses. The Wharton School of Finance and Commerce at the University of Pennsylvania began in 1881. Not until 1900, however, was there even a handful of similar programs at schools such as the University of Chicago, Dartmouth, the University of California, and New York University. Harvard created its Graduate School of Business in 1908.

Harvard, like Dartmouth, required full-time business study, as opposed to the part-time offerings at New York University and many other institutions. The first college textbook in management was published in 1911, a year in which there were thirty different college-level programs in education.

When Dale Carnegie arrived in New York in 1912, the need for business and management training was great. New York was the manufacturing and commercial center not only of the country, but of the world. Few individuals managing the multitude of businesses making up this economic juggernaut had prior business training. Nor did they have much opportunity to find it in New York. This was the need that Carnegie was distinctively able to fill.

THE OPPORTUNITIES FOR LEADERSHIP

Carnegie's response to the needs of his students at the YMCA led him to develop two beliefs about leadership. He was certain that the average person had far more opportunity to benefit from increasing his or her leadership skills than from improving public-speaking skills. And he believed that leadership skills could be developed through education, not just inherited from an old-boy network of people who understood the mysteries of such things.

Carnegie offered his class members practical leadership skills that they could use in their jobs. The course still has this pragmatic orientation. But the *kind* of leadership that Carnegie promoted is much more accepted today than it was seventy-five years ago.

When Carnegie began teaching, the myth of management was all-powerful. The myth was that when a boss said, "Jump," the answer was, "How high?" In 1899, the popular author Elbert Hubbard wrote an essay called "A Message to Garcia." This message of a few hundred words was reprinted over 40 million times and was often distributed by employers to their employees. Carnegie also included it in his own public-speaking texts. Hubbard captured the turn-of-the-century ideal of how employees should respond to leadership. The story was simple. During the Spanish-American war, President McKinley needed to contact quickly Garcia, the leader of the insurgents. Hubbard wrote:

> Garcia was somewhere in the mountain fastnesses of Cuba—no one knew where. No mail or telegraph message could reach him. The President must secure his cooperation, and quickly.
>
> What to do?
>
> Some one said to the President, "There is a fellow by the name of Rowan who will find Garcia for you, if anybody can."

The point I wish to make is this: McKinley gave Rowan a letter to be delivered to Garcia; Rowan took the letter and did not ask, "Where is he at?"

The world was in sore need, Hubbard concluded, of the kind of man:

... who does his work when the "boss" is away, as well as when he is at home.... Civilization is one long, anxious search for just such individuals.... The world cries out for such: he is needed and needed badly—the man who can "Carry a Message to Garcia."

The self-directed, self-starting Rowan may have personified the myth. Yet Carnegie, like Hubbard, realized that such individuals who would do exactly what a boss hoped were in short supply. Carnegie also realized as he developed his course that business was changing the roles of both employees and employers. Businesses were creating large quantities of middle managers. Often well educated, these managers had the somewhat confusing responsibilities of being both a subordinate and a boss. The need to teach the middle manager how to gain the cooperation of those who worked for them took precedence over living up to any dreams of instant obedience.

A manager like Charles Schwab, who had what Carnegie perceived as a genius for management, did not have a staff of automatons ready to jump at his bidding. Schwab, who made Bethlehem Steel the leading manufacturer of steel for the Allies in World War I, relied on his personal skills rather than the power of his position to motivate his workers. Carnegie lionized Schwab as one of two men to receive a salary of a million dollars a year (Walter Chrysler was the other).

Charles Schwab was America's first famous professional manager. To Dale Carnegie, Schwab earned his salary by his ability to deal with people, not his knowledge of steel. Schwab's secret? Positive reinforcement. Schwab prided himself on not criticizing his workers, but using praise to arouse enthusiasm. "I am hearty in my approbation and lavish in my praise," was Schwab's characterization of his method. Carnegie thought it such a useful technique that he cited it four times in *How to Win Friends*.

Carnegie was not alone in identifying and responding to changes in the philosophy and style of leadership. In 1935, a lecturer in personnel administration at Columbia University named Ordway Tead published *The Art of Leadership*. This was an influential and thoughtful work, one that McGraw-Hill went on to reprint more than twenty times. Tead, like Carnegie a year later in *How to Win Friends*, cited Schwab. They both used the anecdote about Schwab increasing production by instilling a sense of competition. In Tead's version:

> Who natively yearns to sweat and struggle to turn out as many tons of steel as possible in eight hours? Yet let a Charlie Schwab walk through the plant and chalk up in a prominent place the number of "heats" turned out by one shift, and those on the next shift may be moved to unprecedented exertion to better that figure.

Although Schwab came into the steel industry when the ideas of scientific management were in full force, he never embraced them. Instead, he—like Dale Carnegie after him—relied on the human side of management. In 1901, Schwab took over Bethlehem Steel. Frederick Taylor, the father of "scientific management," based on measurements of worker output, had up to then been achieving spectacular results at Bethlehem. So spectacular, in fact, that he was going to be able to reduce the work force to about one-fourth of what it had been. This reduction upset the owners, who did not wish to depopulate South Bethlehem where they owned all the houses and the company stores. So when Schwab took control, he ordered the Taylor system to be abandoned. When production fell, some lower-level supervisors went back to Taylor's ideas, deceiving Schwab by saying their practices were not based on Taylorism. Productivity was restored.

To Taylor, the key was finding the most economical way to perform each task. The scientific manager broke down each task into specific operations, then calculated the most efficient way to perform each operation. In Taylor's view, methods were more important than men; once a factory reorganized according to his principles of efficiency, it would virtually run itself without management.

Schwab disagreed with Taylor's methods. To Schwab, it was the leader that made the difference. Leadership meant influencing people to cooperate toward some goal which they came to find desirable. The effective leader did not have to dominate or exploit.

Both Tead and Carnegie cited Schwab because Schwab knew *how* to lead. The effective leader knows how to transmit his energy to his followers. He can replace commands with delegation. He knows how to deal effectively with people on an individual basis. These skills could be taught.

Both authors also used Owen Young of General Electric as an example of an effective executive who asked questions instead of giving orders. It was not mollycoddling employees to treat them courteously. Similarly, it was preferable to criticize in private and to give "two pats on the back for one kick in the pants."

LEARNING TO BE A LEADER: GETTING PEOPLE TO LIKE YOU

To Carnegie, there were essentially three levels of leadership. The first, and easiest, was getting people to like you. The concept sounds basic, but many people are never taught how to do it.

Take, for instance, Peter Albrecht, a recent graduate of a prestigious business school. Smart, hard-working, and capable, he could not understand why he was being ignored by his colleagues at a large advertising agency. He had heard about the MBA syndrome, where graduate students newly minted as Masters of Business Administration had trouble fitting into organizations, but he hadn't imagined it happening to him. Albrecht had enrolled in the Carnegie course to sharpen his presentation skills. When it came time to make a commitment to become a friendlier person, he chose to apply the principles at the office.

His strategy was simple. He would try to be friendlier in the morning. Instead of rushing in at 8:30 and heading straight for his office to enjoy a cup of coffee and review his mail, he would make a point of smiling at people, greeting them by name and spending a little time chatting. This was the only conscious change he tried to make in his behavior. But after three weeks, he felt he was starting to fit in more. Don, from down the hall, had pointed out to him a project deadline that he had been unaware of. Albrecht would have looked bad if he hadn't met it. Tom, another account executive, asked him to join in a new client presentation that had exciting potential.

Albrecht found himself looking forward to coming to the office. "Maybe these things would have happened anyway," he told the class when he reported on his commitment. "But I don't think so. So, if you want to have a better time at work, use people's names. And smile."

Nancy Arbor is another class member who found that working at being a friendlier person made a difference in the way she felt about her job. The credit manager in a large publishing company, she had been in her job for over five years. She was good at it and thought she enjoyed it, but was frustrated that most of her contact with people was over the phone. There was significant turnover in her company, so she decided to take it upon herself to introduce herself to every newly hired person on her floor. The day someone started, she would stop in for ten or fifteen minutes, get acquainted, and answer questions about the company.

The results? She felt good doing it because people seemed so appreciative that she had made the effort. She also felt that it was nicer to be able to walk down the halls and know who everybody was. Plus, one of the new employees ended up a last-minute replacement for a share in the summer house Nancy rented with four other women.

Smiling, not criticizing, using people's names, being a good listener, giving sincere appreciation are the commonsense techniques that Carnegie advocated to become a friendlier person.

Once class members become exposed to the techniques, they usually find them easy and worthwhile to follow.

Establishing a friendly rapport is only the first of three leadership levels in the Carnegie method. The second level is gaining someone's cooperation.

HOW TO GAIN ENTHUSIASTIC COOPERATION

American business seems plagued by bosses who have a very low opinion of the productivity of their secretaries and administrative assistants. Frequently, the attitude is returned. Or so you might conclude from sitting in on Dale Carnegie classes.

When class members make a commitment to gain someone's enthusiastic cooperation, they're often talking about job-related activities. A boss, for instance, resolves to get his or her secretary to do a better job by beginning in a friendly way. He might let the secretary feel that the idea is his or her own, or might throw down a challenge. For many, these resolutions signify a departure from the "when I say jump, please jump" school of management.

Class member Al Benjamin was put out with his secretary Janine. Her typing was full of errors. She rushed out at 5:00 no matter what Al still had to accomplish. She was behind in her filing. They barely spoke to each other, and Al was about to call personnel to ask for a replacement.

But he decided to try some of the Carnegie principles. He started making a point of asking Janine about her family and her hobby of designing clothes. He looked for things he could praise in her work. And one day at 4:30 when a project was dumped on his desk to be done by the next morning, he asked Janine for her suggestions as to how he could get it done.

After talking for several minutes about alternatives, Janine suddenly said, "You know, that's silly. I can get it done faster myself. I'll do it." So she stayed until 7:00 and finished it. Looking back at his experience, Al said the improvement in Janine's work pleased him and that working together had become much more pleasant.

Charlie Thompson was pleased with his ability to get enthusiastic cooperation. He applied the principles at home with his twelve-year-old son Paul. For months Charlie had been after Paul to clean up his room and help with the dishes. He reasoned, he yelled, he threatened to cut off his son's allowance. Nothing worked.

Feeling he had nothing to lose, Charlie decided to try the principles. "I decided," Charlie told the class, "to try and see things from Paul's point of view.

"And rather than lecturing Paul, I decided to get him to talk to me. So we went out for hamburgers, something the two of us hadn't done for years by ourselves. I asked Paul how things were going, and he started to open up a bit to me. I hadn't realized how pressured he was feeling about trying to do well in soccer and keep his grades up. The kid really felt overwhelmed.

"I realized that he wasn't being malicious about his room; he just couldn't focus on it. I told him that I didn't want to make a big deal out of his room. We weren't trying to run a boot camp. But I told him that his mother wanted to keep it decent. If he could put his dirty clothes in the hamper, rather than all over the floor, it would make her life easier. I asked Paul to remember that his mother was working and felt the same kind of pressure he did.

"Paul's room isn't the world's neatest now," Charlie said. "But it's a definite improvement. And what I didn't expect is that the two of us are talking more than we have for years."

In Carnegie's view, leadership skills were required of every mother, father, wife, and husband. He realized that for many people the greatest opportunity to flex new leadership skills was on the home front. And results at home could mean more than changes at the office.

CHANGING ATTITUDES
AND BEHAVIOR

The third and toughest level of leadership is changing some-one's attitude or behavior. Sometimes this is the same as getting a lackadaisical worker to become an enthusiastic worker. Other times it has nothing to do with enthusiasm. An effective instructor will demonstrate how to change someone's behavior through his or her teaching techniques. For although Carnegie didn't want his instructors to criticize, he did expect them to change behavior in class members.

John Stevens tells a story about an accident that happened on a summer vacation. In the first thirty seconds of his two-minute talk, he sets the scene chopping wood at a campground by Vermont's Lake Champlain. But he is not getting into the story fast enough. His instructor, Robin Peters, speaks up from the back of the room:

"John, strong topic, but now *show* us."

John begins to pantomime swinging the ax. She encourages him, "That's it—good action."

John acts out the story and holds the class's attention. When he sits down, Robin asks, "Did you feel how much more natural and effective you were when you started acting out the story?"

Robin's coaching technique was an example of several of the techniques Carnegie advocated for changing people. She began with praise ("strong topic"). She led John to put more action into his talk. Then she closed with encouragement and praise. Some instructors call this the sandwich technique: Praise goes on both sides of constructive criticism. The technique works primarily because a skillful instructor makes the class member feel happy through recognizing that the change is an improvement.

Toward the end of the course's fourteen sessions, class members make a commitment to change someone's attitude or behavior. The choices are almost endless. A boss resolves to put an error-prone trainee at ease by talking about all the mistakes he made when he was started. A twenty-eight-year-old owner of a duplex decides to surprise her upstairs tenants by being very friendly and asking them if it wouldn't be more sensible to turn the thermostat down than to open the window. The mother of a teenage boy is going to stop nagging her son about studying. She's going to seek ways she can use positive reinforcement.

As class members report successful experiences in changing people's behavior and attitudes, they achieve a greater sense of control. They observe that it is possible to accomplish changes that previously might have seemed unattainable. They also see that the process must begin with setting a goal that has a payoff for everyone.

For instance, both the boss and the trainee will benefit if the trainee makes fewer errors. Why should the boss try to score points at the expense of the trainee or make him feel badly? Just finding fault is unlikely to improve overall performance.

Principles such as "Call attention to people's mistakes indirectly," and "Let the other person save face," sound like common sense. They appear brand new, however, to many class members. Business education is far more popular today than when Carnegie started his course. Nonetheless, very few undergraduate or MBA programs teach these mundane details of how to deal with people.

You won't find a copy of *How to Win Friends* at Harvard Business School's Baker Library, the largest business library in the country. Until recently, there wasn't even a course at Harvard that dealt with the importance of interpersonal relationships and leadership. Then, Professor John Kotter introduced a course called "Power and Influence." Not surprisingly, the course became very popular, for it recognized that doing well in leadership jobs, regardless of level or formal title, required paying attention to relationships and the process of getting cooperation.

Kotter's course and his book, also called *Power and Influence*, encourage people to think about work in terms of their relationships at work and to recognize the significance of leadership issues. But he stops short of providing nuts-and-bolts suggestions for implementing the ideas. In other words, he makes the student and reader consider the key question. How do you learn to lead?

Only recently are writers on management focusing on the nitty-gritty. Thomas J. Peters, who has achieved extraordinary popularity through books such as *In Search of Excellence*, *A Passion for Excellence*, and *Thriving on Chaos*, does give advice on how a manager should lead. Like Carnegie, he gives a shopping list of simple principles that anyone can use to deal with the people in the office.

Today, middle managers must typically concern themselves with their relationships with peers, with people in other departments and divisions, and with people outside the company. Many jobs require complex leadership skills. At lower levels there may be fewer people to manage, but there is also likely to be less formal authority. So the individual who has developed his or her leadership skills has increasing value to the organization.

The Carnegie course does not pay much attention to management theory. Theory X and Theory Y; MBO (Management by Objectives); ZBB (zero-based budgeting); CPM (Critical Path Method); and other techniques of management science never get mentioned. The principles of leadership used in the course have not changed since Carnegie first published them in 1936. But the recognition in corporate America that the course gets people to change the way they deal with other people is a major reason corporations pay for 75 percent of tuitions and that Carnegie course business has boomed in recent years.

CHAPTER 7

FROM PUBLIC SPEAKING TO HUMAN RELATIONS

1913: I have only words of commendation for Mr. Carnagey's public speaking course. When one considers how brief the time, and how very moderate the price, one marvels that so much is accomplished. By making me think on my feet and by practice, Mr. Carnagey did me a world of good.

Edward M. Keator
Attorney

1987: I signed up for the Dale Carnegie course because I became president of the board of trustees of my son's private school. I was scared half to death by the prospect of not only having to run meetings, but having to address the whole school.

Commencement was two weeks after the course ended, and I gave a fifteen-minute talk. And you know something? I felt pretty comfortable giving it. I didn't write out my speech, but just used some brief notes. It really wasn't any harder than talking in class, and I felt I was able to get my points across. We have to raise a lot of money, and I was able to speak with conviction. I think I convinced people that we have challenges ahead of us, but they're ones we can meet.

Paul Harris
New York City businessman

BE YOURSELF

You can boil down Dale Carnegie's principles of effective speaking to two words: Be yourself. The difficulty is not in understanding the directions, but in implementing them. A novice speaker following the Carnegie method essentially is learning to avoid depending on technique. Instead, the speaker adopts a style similar to the way he would speak informally to a friend or colleague seated on the other side of a desk. That process of freeing yourself from a particular set of techniques is similar to what Carnegie himself went through in the forty-two years he taught the course.

When he started teaching public speaking at the YMCA, Carnegie relied on the same formal techniques he had learned in college back in Warrensburg, Missouri. He used classic speakers such as Edmund Burke, William Pitt, and Daniel Webster as models to imitate. Realizing that his classes of businessmen were not the least interested in learning how to recite "Horatius at the Bridge," he abandoned the old role models. He got class members speaking on topics they cared about. He kept for many years, however, his reliance on techniques of public speaking.

In 1915, he coauthored a textbook with J. Berg Esenwein called *The Art of Public Speaking*. This emphasized technique. The authors admitted that public speaking was something you learned by doing and for which experience was not only the best teacher, but the first and last. Then they went on to produce more than five hundred pages of material. Chapters included The Sin of Monotony, Efficiency through Change of Pitch, Distinctiveness and Precision of Utterance, The Truth about Gesture ("If you are troubled by your gestures or a lack of gestures, attend to the cause, not the effect"), and voice charm.

Voice charm meant musical, joyous tones, which nasal resonance could achieve. Not, the authors warned, a nasal tone, but "the true nasal quality which is so well illustrated by the voice work of trained French singers and speakers." If the reader was still unsure, Esenwein and Carnegie advised him to practice singing out "ding-dong ... Hong-Kong" emphasizing the *ng* sounds with brightness. They also suggested reading lyric poems, such as Milton's "L'Allegro" and Tennyson's "The Brook," as a technique for putting the "smile and joy of soul into your voice."

There were also seven chapters on different ways to exert influence. The techniques of influence ranged from exposition (which included rhetorical techniques such as contrast and antithesis, analogy, division, and generalization) to description, narration (emphasizing the anecdote), suggestion, argument, and persuasion. The authors also discussed techniques of influencing the crowd, which, they agreed, was critical in business:

> Success in business, in the last analysis, turns upon touching the imagination of crowds. The reason that preachers in this present generation are less successful in getting people to want goodness than business men are in getting them to want motorcars, hats, and pianolas, is that business men as a class ... have boned down harder to the art of touching the imaginations of the crowds.

Additionally, 20 percent of the book reprinted speeches for study and practice, including: Henry Watterson on "The New Americanism" (abridged); Robert Toombs' 1861 speech "On Resigning from the Senate"; Theodore Roosevelt's "On American Motherhood"; and William Jennings Bryan's "The Prince of Peace." Bryan's speech included this notable passage:

I do not carry the doctrine of evolution as far as some do; I am not yet convinced that man is a lineal descendant of the lower animals. I do not mean to find fault with you if you want to accept the theory; all I mean to say is that while you may trace your ancestry back to the monkey if you find pleasure or pride in doing so, you shall not connect me with your family tree without more evidence than has yet been produced.

For Carnegie, being coauthor of the book in 1915 was a chance to break into print and establish his credentials as an instructor. In 1926, with eleven years additional teaching experience, he wrote by himself *Public Speaking: A Practical Course for the Businessman*, a text that the Carnegie course used until 1962. Today, in substantially revised form with much less emphasis on technique, it remains one of the three textbooks in the course.

PUBLIC SPEAKING PRINCIPLES

When Carnegie wrote *Public Speaking* in 1926, his course was still essentially one in public speaking. The emphasis on human relations was yet to come. There were sixteen chapters in the text, one for each session of the course. The opening chapters stressed developing courage and self-confidence; they were followed by chapters on delivery, platform presence, openings, and closes. Speech-building exercises, which included lessons on word pronunciation and breathing, supplemented each chapter. The book ended with a chapter on improving diction, followed by reprints of two famous speeches, "Acres of Diamonds" by Russell Conwell and "As a Man Thinketh" by James Allen, and Elbert Hubbard's tract "A Message to Garcia."

Although a reader might easily get bogged down in all the exercises, Dale Carnegie's basic approach to speaking was present underneath all the how-to technique. By 1926, he had identified enthusiasm as the key to effective speaking. He had more faith in the spirit of public speaking than in its rules. He also was advising not to memorize talks word for word, a principle the course continues to emphasize.

By the early 1930s, he had further refined his thinking on the teaching of public speaking. In 1932, he told an interviewer for *The American Magazine* about his methods of teaching businessmen to think and talk on their feet. This was the same magazine for which he himself had written articles such as "Show Windows that Sell Goods" and "Money Made in Writing for the Movies" almost twenty years earlier when he was still known as Dale Carnagey. He told the interviewer:

> Public speaking really cannot be *taught*. Do you think, if I lectured a boy for fifty hours, I could teach him how to swim? He has to teach himself. All I can do is lead him down into the water and try to give him confidence.
> Learning to speak in public is like learning to swim. The best teacher in both is practice, and the greatest obstacle to both is fear.

He went on to describe how the first six sessions of the course were sufficient to free a class member from stage fright. Then in the balance of the course, the class member could have fun and learn some of the principles and rules of public speaking.

When pressed during the interview to describe these principles, Carnegie admitted that over the years he had lost his faith in rules. Instead, he now relied on a series of common-sense principles. The key principle was to talk about what the speaker knows and cares about so he or she can speak with sincerity and enthusiasm. The other guidelines included: Prepare a speech thoroughly, but don't memorize or read it aloud. Use an attention-getting opening and be sure to end your talk before your audience wants you to. Avoid humor unless you're a natural humorist. And: Speak directly to and with your audience.

THE FUNDAMENTALS
OF SPEAKING

Through the years, Carnegie held a growing conviction that the fundamentals were what counted. Good public speaking is merely enlarged conversation, he would write, but it is a sure way to leadership. The basic questions he answered for Rotarians are the same questions class members voice two generations later.

What shall I talk about? As millions of Dale Carnegie graduates have learned, talk about what interests you. If you can speak with enthusiasm, you will be sure to interest your audience.

How shall I prepare? Spend an hour of preparation for every seven seconds you expect to talk, he told the Rotarians. In time, he became more realistic about the time people would devote to preparation. He never lost his conviction, however, that a speaker must earn the right to speak by knowing a subject before talking about it. That preparation could come from life experiences or library research, but in each case the speaker needed real knowledge. He couldn't fake it.

How can I organize my material? Carnegie advised focusing first on the idea you want to convey and developing illustrations to make it clear, interesting, and vivid. Then create an attention-getting opening and an impressive closing.

What gestures shall I make? Don't worry about making any gestures, Carnegie suggested. The audience doesn't need them. Nevertheless, spontaneous animation often helps the speaker relax and be more naturally enthusiastic.

Shall I put my hands in my pockets? If Teddy Roosevelt and William Jennings Bryan did it, it was all right by Dale Carnegie. If you didn't feel comfortable with your hands by your sides, the most appropriate place for them, putting them in your pockets was acceptable.

Shall I memorize my talk? The answer was unequivocal: "No! Never!" A few brief notes were acceptable. (Carnegie himself often wrote one-word cues to himself on cards that he used during his longer speeches).

How long shall I talk? Stop before your audience wants you to, advised Carnegie. Abraham Lincoln took less than five minutes for the Gettysburg Address. You should not take more than ten minutes for your talk unless you are much better than you think you are.

In 1949, when Carnegie summed up his philosophy of public speaking for a magazine article, he did not mention any oratorical techniques that he had once learned and then taught others. There were no instructions on how to make flowing, half-circle gestures or when to grasp your jacket lapels to look important. Instead, his focus was on substance. His most important tip was to prepare thoroughly. He instructed his readers to talk on topics born from years of work or life experience.

His other secrets included: Don't write out your talks. Never memorize a talk word for word. Fill your talk with illustrations and examples. Rehearse your speech by conversing with your friends. "Instead of worrying about your delivery," he said, "get busy with the causes that produce it." And finally, don't try imitating others; be yourself.

In today's classes, students continue to speak on their feet in every session. After session five, however, the instructor does not focus on delivery. As Carnegie found years ago, people often become comfortable as speakers in a few sessions. They lose the nervous gestures, the awkward pauses, the stiffness, and internal fear that had made public speaking so painful.

THE PROBLEM OF SINCERITY

A warm, supportive environment where people were increasing their confidence was certainly a healthy one for both Carnegie and his students. There the lonely actor and would-be

author—also, at this point, a bachelor—discovered a classroom
world that nurtured him as much as he nurtured it. The more
students flocked to his courses, applauded his methods, and
in time purchased his books, the more secure their instructor
became.

Eventually this farmer, salesman, actor, teacher, and role
model who was Dale Carnegie came head to head with a persistent problem: Where was the sincerity in all this speech-giving,
role-playing, testimonial-giving, and acting? Most people could
act enthusiastic long enough to convince the boss and get a
promotion and raise. But unless you were genuinely and sincerely enthusiastic, eventually both those around you—and you
yourself—would see through the part.

Carnegie handled the problem of sincerity somewhat glibly,
but at least he considered the issue important enough to address.
Filled with the memories of the tens of thousands of talks he
had heard, Carnegie believed that anyone could detect insincerity. After all, you could immediately tell in his course when
someone was giving a talk from the heart as opposed to rehashing
a magazine article.

Understanding sincerity was as simple as judging the difference between appreciation and flattery. "That is simple. One
comes from the heart out; the other from the teeth out. One is
unselfish; the other selfish." Being sincere was like smiling. If
you did it, you soon enough would believe it. Once again, feeling
would follow action.

Some critics of his early classes thought he was creating cadres
of glad-handing, manipulative go-getters. His graduates were
supposedly going to claw their way to the top at the expense of
those innocent folks who hadn't learned the Carnegie way. Several critics attended one or two sessions in the course, but none
went through the entire fourteen meetings.

The course has a disarming effect on participants. After a few
sessions, although some may consider it too much like a pep
rally, virtually no one views it as insincere. If anything, observers
sometimes feel the classroom is reeking with sincerity. Carnegie
recognized early in his career that very few people are skilled

enough at acting to feign sincerity. And most listeners are very skilled at intuitively detecting insincerity. He didn't teach people to try to fool anybody.

At the same time, however, his assumptions about sincerity sometimes let him come across as quite naive. In *How to Win Friends*, for example, he portrays John D. Rockefeller, Jr., bringing a bloody, bitter, two-year strike to a happy end by approaching the strikers in a friendly fashion. His friendliness, Carnegie argued, caused the strikers to go back to work without saying another word about the wage increase for which they had struck.

In truth, Carnegie was playing a bit loose with the facts. Rockefeller did in fact address the workers in a direct and confident fashion. Nevertheless, it was the substance of the solution he presented (specific agreements on wages and working and living conditions and an innovative employee representation plan) that persuaded the strikers to vote for it.

Although the anecdote is not accurate, the distortion reflects Carnegie's beliefs. He believed that Rockefeller had prevailed because of a skillful use of human-relations principles. To Carnegie, a peaceful settlement of the strike spelled success, no matter what the workers might receive for a wage increase. The outcome wasn't as important as the method. If the workers had doubled their wages in an equally friendly manner, Carnegie would still have called the meeting with Rockefeller a success.

BOOTSTRAP PHILOSOPHY

The problem of being cheerful caught up with Dale Carnegie in the midst of the Depression. Flushed with his own success in surviving, he took his own experience as proof that anyone could pull himself out of poverty or mental depression. If people failed, it was their own fault. An inspirational article he wrote for *Colliers* magazine in 1938 was entitled, simply, "Grab Your Bootstraps." Writing the year before John Steinbeck published

The Grapes of Wrath, Carnegie might well have been living in a different world:

> I don't know the figures, but I doubt if ten people a year starve to death in the United States. That is, if they do not wish to do so. Of course, some do; they have too much pride, or some other bit of foolishness, and calmly sit down and await the end. Food is everywhere in this amazing land of ours. All we have to do is to go to the right authorities and ask for it.

The Missouri farmboy had forgotten what poverty was like. Carnegie did provide some specific advice to face "these troublous times." Talk encouragement, he wrote, when your friends talk discouragement. Don't think about your troubles at night. Act as if you were not afraid. And, keep physically fit. The more discouraged you are, the more golf you should play.

In a *Saturday Evening Post* interview, the reporter observed that Carnegie "sees the world as a place full of people eternally struggling against fearful odds, groping in a vast darkness haunted by specters. A successful man, to him, is a stout-hearted man who is prepared for the worst."

Carnegie was successful, but always prepared for disaster. As the reporter noted, he once asked a man if he was completely happy, and when the man replied "Yes," Carnegie "unleashed a flood of incredulity upon the happy pupil."

Although Carnegie recognized that he made his living from other people's unhappiness, he also believed he made life better for them. Seeing the results of his classes confirmed that belief. But personal doubts remained, largely because he never really reconciled his own confusion of motives. Was he a writer who fell into the habit of teaching? Or a missionary in the savage world of business? Was his gospel one of doing good for others? Or of looking out for yourself? Was success his real goal? Or was it to be the albatross around his neck? He was not one to search deeply for answers. Nonetheless, the urge to find some expression for these doubts is certainly evident in his writings.

TODAY'S BENEFITS

Dale Carnegie would have felt comfortable with modern-day psychologists of the "I'm okay, you're okay," transactional analysis school. Although he didn't use terms like winners and ego states, his end of self-realization was also to create winners. A winner is defined in transactional analysis terms as an authentic person who doesn't try to be something he or she imagines he should be. Instead, winners are themselves. Winners don't use their energy putting on a performance, maintaining a pretense, and manipulating others. Winners are able to reveal themselves instead of projecting images that please or provoke others.

In the Dale Carnegie classroom, every class member is considered a success. Each is a winner. Public speaking is a way that people learn to be themselves. By revealing himself in the secure environment of the classroom, the successful class member develops the confidence to be more comfortable in the real world as well.

Carnegie's approach has many similarities to that of Benjamin Franklin, an important model for him. Largely because of his role as Poor Richard, Franklin has an image of someone who will lead you to riches. Franklin wrote:

> In short, the way to wealth, if you desire it, is as plain as the way to market. It depends chiefly on two words, *industry* and *frugality*; that is, waste neither time nor money, but make the best use of both. He that gets all he can honestly, and saves all he gets (necessary expenses excepted) will certainly become *Rich*.

The key phrase may be "if you desire it." Franklin didn't follow his own advice for getting wealth. He essentially retired at forty-two and used the money he had made in business to support a host of other endeavors, from science to diplomacy to education. Although he decided that he himself did not desire wealth, he did not repudiate it as a goal for others.

Similarly, Carnegie never sought riches nor indulged himself when they fell in his lap, but he did not have trouble recommending financial rewards as a goal. His textbook on public speaking, for instance, reprinted Russell Conwell's famous speech "Acres of Diamonds." Carnegie used this remarkable speech in two ways. First, it was an outstanding example of knowing one's audience. Conwell delivered this speech almost six thousand times and still tailored it to the interests of each group. Second, Carnegie used the speech as an inspiration to class members to get out and mine the diamonds in their own backyards—their own personal qualities and skills as human beings. As Conwell advised an audience in his home town of Philadelphia:

> I say you ought to be rich; you have no right to be poor. To live in Philadelphia and not be rich is a misfortune, and it is doubly a misfortune, because you could have been rich just as well as poor. Philadelphia furnishes so many opportunities. You ought to be rich.... You and I know there are some things more valuable than money; of course, we do. Ah, yes! By a heart made unspeakably sad by a grave on which the autumn leaves now fall, I know there are some things higher and grander and sublimer than money. Well does the man know, who has suffered, that there are some things sweeter and holier and more sacred than gold. Nevertheless, the man of common sense also knows that there is not any one of these things that is not greatly enhanced by the use of money. Money is power.

SETTING GOALS

To Carnegie, like Conwell, other things were ostensibly more important than money and material success. In *How to Stop Worrying*, for example, Carnegie bemoans the way many businessmen who control their tongues at the office will speak harshly to their wives. "Yet," Carnegie writes, "for their personal happiness, marriage is far more important to them, far more vital, than business."

As in Carnegie's day, a significant portion of the course in the 1980s revolves around the process of setting goals. Class members decide what is important to them individually. Then the class provides the framework for goal-setting and the motivation to achieve a desired success.

Long before Dale Carnegie, Henry David Thoreau declared, "In the long run men hit only what they aim at." But it is startling how many people come to the course never before having set short- or long-term goals for themselves.

The specific careers and professions described by people today are much different from fifty years ago. The process of setting goals, however, is much the same. The personal goals that class members set at the end of the course are the indicators of what success means to them. Is it financial returns? Material possessions? Peace of mind?

At the last session of the course, class members verbalize their most important personal goal for the next year. The goals of a recent class in New York City reflect how class members do not fall into lockstep when it comes to defining success. The course does create an atmosphere in which people spend time thinking about what is important to them and what they are willing to make a commitment to go after. Here are some examples of class members and their diverse goals:

- A magazine production coordinator who wants to get along better with people at work.
- A liquor store owner who wants to lose weight.
- A computer saleswoman who wants to find a new apartment.
- A stockbroker who wants to make more cold calls and generate more business.
- An architect who wants to set up a partnership so he can work with other people.
- A lawyer who wants to find a new job.

- An advertising account executive who wants to learn to play golf, so she can play with her father.
- A computer technician who wants to make time to read books.
- A small company executive who wants to increase employee productivity.
- A bond trader who wants to take up speed walking as regular exercise.
- An Indian entrepreneur who wants to work with Mother Teresa.
- A textile saleswoman who wants to learn how to manage the money she's earning from a recent increase in salary.
- A building materials salesman who wants his boss's job.
- A nurse who wants to control her worries about her brother who has AIDS.
- An unemployed woman who wants to start writing again.
- An office equipment saleswoman who wants to become an actress as a hobby.
- A computer salesman who wants to be able to tell his father he loves him.
- A young, middle-level manager who wants to become enthusiastic about moving with her company to another part of the country.

Dale Carnegie's focus on success reflected the middle-class values of his era. He expected his graduates to live a life reflecting their own values, which would probably be those of the middle class. To Dale Carnegie, a successful graduate would have more self confidence and a repertoire of human-relations principles. These would enable him or her to be a more effective leader. How the graduates used the confidence and leadership skills was up to them.

CHAPTER 8

FROM CARNEGIE HALL TO COVENT GARDEN

T RUE TO THE RESOLUTION THAT HE HAD MADE FOR himself in 1912 ("I want to live to write and write to live"), Dale Carnegie persevered in his writing career.

In 1913, Carnegie took a writing course at the Columbia University School of Journalism. The following year, he took a short-story writing course at New York University. His writing professor gave him an A and predicted that Carnegie would become a success.

As he'd hoped, Carnegie was soon making enough teaching night school to support himself and also pursue his writing. He postponed whatever novels he had in mind to turn out articles that eventually appeared in popular general-interest magazines of the day, including *World Outlook, The American Magazine, Pictorial Review,* and *Illustrated World.*

Among the first articles was "How I Laid the Foundation for a Big Salary" (*The American Magazine,* August, 1916). This was the story of a man who started as a handy-boy in a bank in his home town and, by working hard, eventually became corporation president, earning $60,000 a year. It was a typical rags-to-riches story.

Carnegie undoubtedly saw his own career aspirations reflected in the young man who soared to power by dint of long hours of hard work. "I plunged into my new duties aflame with enthusiasm," the successful businessman told the young reporter, "to send this bank's business barometer skyrocketing, to strike a rapid, decisive blow—that was my ambition. . . . I pleaded for cooperation, and tried patiently to fire [my employees] with vision and enthusiasm."

For *Illustrated World,* Carnegie wrote a feature article on Sir Douglas Mawson, an Antarctic explorer. In 1911, Mawson was one of three men who ventured several hundred miles into King George V Land. One companion died when his sledge plunged into a crevasse, carrying away most of the provisions and fuel. After two weeks on the ice, Mawson's second companion died of starvation and cold. Mawson continued alone. His "unshakable determination" saved his life, Carnegie observed. "Worry about himself would have sapped the energy that carried him through."

If Carnegie learned about enthusiasm from business leaders and determination from Antarctic explorers, he learned the lesson of "instilling an eager want" from champion money-raiser C. S. Ward. In *World Outlook* Carnegie described Ward as a man who touched on civic pride, enthusiasm, and the "joy that comes from self-sacrifice" to raise money for various causes. Ward's advice has a distinct Carnegie flavor to it: "If you want to make people act, aim a few inches below their collarbone on the left side—that is where they do most of their thinking."

New inventions of the day also caught the interest of the young journalist. Most notable among these was a curious attitude-testing device invented by a Dr. von David. The device operated somewhat like a biofeedback machine. Words were projected on a screen in front of a subject. Dr. von David's machine used a small voltmeter to measure the person's response to each word. Carnegie was fascinated by the results of the experimental tests:

> If the suggestive words upon the screen result in quick, clear, exhilarating mental processes, the emotional secretions show exaltation; but if these suggestive words cause no pleasure, only sluggish thoughts and poor concentration, the emotional secretions register depression. It is a truism old as war that we accomplish our best work under the influence of pleasure and exaltation. When the work is really enjoyable, concentration, enthusiasm, and the impulse to achieve are strengthened.

Dr. von David's testing machine led Carnegie to the conclusion that words were a powerful psychological force that could produce instant results of extreme pleasure or depression. In this device Carnegie saw his own theories of human behavior scientifically proved.

The magazine assignments provided Carnegie with choice opportunities to meet famous and interesting people, inquire into methods for achieving success, and explore ideas or inventions that intrigued him. His appearance in the popular press assured him that he was, in fact, a publishable writer.

His articles have the breathless tone of someone just meeting wonderfully exciting people and encountering awe-inspiring inventions for the first time. He was appealing to readers' tastes in the prewar equivalents of *People* magazine. Moreover, writing these articles gave him formative lessons in the kind of prose that would appeal to a broad, popular audience.

Carnegie began to experiment with various ways of catching the reader's attention in the lead paragraph of an article. "America's Champion Money Raiser" begins with a thoughtful quote from a famous person:

"The only thing that saves the world," according to President Wilson, "is the little handful of disinterested men who are in it."

That philosophy makes C. S. Ward a world savior; he is most ardently disinterested in himself.

Another approach that appealed to Carnegie was the narrative of success. "How I Laid the Foundation for a Big Salary (As Told to Dale Carnagey)" begins with the following:

From my first job as a handy-boy about a bank in my home town at a wage of $15 a month, up to my present position as president of a corporation at $60,000 a year, there is a trail so clear that today I can almost check off every step in it.

Carnegie developed a dramatic, overstated style in these early magazine pieces. The same tone of high drama would characterize the style of his later books. Part I, Chapter 1 of *How to Win Friends and Influence People* begins:

On May 7, 1931, the most sensational manhunt New York had ever known had come to its climax. After weeks of search, "Two-Gun" Crowley—the killer, the gunman who didn't smoke or drink—was at bay, trapped in his sweetheart's apartment on West End Avenue.

As an attention-grabber, that beginning is hard to beat. The style is perfect popular magazine, and pure Carnegie. In his early trials as a magazine writer, Carnegie had discovered how to appeal to the largest number of people in the briefest amount of space: Begin dramatically, tell a good story, make a point, and deliver a benefit.

It was a style that would eventually sell millions of books.

Dale Carnegie's birthplace in Harmony Church, ten miles northeast of Maryville, Missouri, was a wood-frame farmhouse on a flood plain near the 102 River. Annual flooding wiped out most years' crops, keeping the Carnegie family in a state of perpetual poverty. Carnegie admired his parents' fortitude through hard times, and he often praised his mother's enduring faith, but chose a career as salesman rather than farmer. (Courtesy, Nodaway County Heritage Collection)

A school portrait of Dale Carnegie (then Carnagey), age six, and his classmates at Rose Hill School in Nodaway County, Missouri in 1894. Always self-conscious about his prominent ears, Dale (seated, front row, fourth from left) appears disgruntled at having his picture taken. His older brother Clifton (standing, third row, fifth from left) is the only other boy wearing a white yoke collar. "Those days," Dale later wrote, "I was ashamed of the fact that I lived on a farm—I was ashamed of our poverty; and the people who lived in Maryville gave me an inferiority complex." (Courtesy, Nodaway County Heritage Collection)

Dale Carnegie began teaching public-speaking courses in 1912 at the 125th Street YMCA in New York, when he was twenty-four. Discouraged with his job as a Packard truck salesman, Carnegie began teaching the course as a way to make money while he worked on a novel. The Y's manager was initially skeptical that anyone would be interested in public speaking, but Carnegie's course became one of the most popular ever offered at the YMCA. Eventually, Carnegie began teaching his program in YMCAs up and down the East Coast. (Courtesy, Archives of the YMCA of Greater New York)

Lowell Thomas, charismatic world traveler and broadcaster, took public-speaking lessons from Dale Carnegie in 1916, only months before setting off for his Middle East adventures with T. E. Lawrence. After World War I, Carnegie helped Lowell Thomas write the script for the London debut of Thomas's stage show, film, and travelogue, *With Allenby in Palestine and Lawrence in Arabia*. In the show, Thomas appeared on stage in typical Arab garb, complete with turban. (Courtesy, Wide World Photos)

In 1930 Dale Carnegie was again called upon to help Lowell Thomas prepare scripts, this time for his nightly newscast on the *Literary Digest*-sponsored program on NBC radio. As America's best-known newscaster, Thomas helped Carnegie by publicly endorsing his courses and writing a preface for the first edition of *How to Win Friends and Influence People*. In later years Carnegie was a frequent visitor to the Lowell Thomas estate in Pawling, New York. (Courtesy, Wide World Photos)

Dale Carnegie at home in Forest Hills in February 1937, three months after publication of *How to Win Friends*. Between January and April of 1937, the book went through thirty printings and 333,000 copies. The modest author had expected to sell about thirty thousand copies, and when the book became a bestseller, Carnegie told a reporter he "was the most surprised man in the world." (Courtesy, Wide World Photos)

First-time speakers overcome by shyness were encouraged to new heights of bravery by Dale Carnegie. In 1938 he was shown holding the arm of a nervous student who struggled to speak into a microphone. Carnegie realized that the courage to speak in public would help students gain greater control of their personal and professional lives. (Courtesy, UPI/Bettmann Newsphotos)

Can You Think Fast On Your Feet?

PHOTOGRAPH BY GEORGE R. PHILLIPS
FOR THE AMERICAN MAGAZINE

Here is one of the tumultuous heckling sessions by which Dale Carnegie trains men to dominate their hearers. Mr. Carnegie, who stands at the left of the harassed speaker, has listened to 150,000 speeches. In this article he passes along some of the helpful things he has learned while teaching executives to speak in public

By JOHN JANNEY

ONE night early this winter thirty of the executives, engineers, and sales managers of a large Philadelphia corporation were gathered in a committee-room. The atmosphere was filled with nervous tension. The senior vice president, a tall, grave, and hitherto highly respected man, rose to speak.

"Gentlemen," he said, "the first great rule of success is hard work. I want . . ."

"Boo-ooh!" was the unanimous response.

"Boo all you want," said the vice president, with attempted calm, "but the fact remains that unless a man rolls up his sleeves . . ."

"In this weather?" demanded the sales manager for the Chicago territory, sneeringly. "Try that on the lake front and catch pneumonia."

The vice president's face was red. He mopped his brow.

"Now, listen, gentlemen," he pleaded. "Give me a chance. It's only fair play to . . ."

"Boo-ooh!" came the hostile roar again. "Throw him out . . . put him out of his misery . . ."

THEY stamped their feet, pounded on tables, shook their fists. The sweat poured from the vice president's brow. His face was now white. And at this un-happy moment a thin, smallish, bespectacled man stepped up behind the once honored vice president, hauled off, and hit him a staggering blow on the back with a tightly folded newspaper.

"Now's your time," he grated. "Snap into it. Let loose the old enthusiasm. Dominate these yapping curs. Go after them. Make them eat out of your hand."

The vice president glared at his adviser, then turned to face his other tormentors. Timidity and nervousness vanished before his rising anger. He fought off his hecklers, made them listen to him, and finished his speech triumphantly.

This discordant meeting was not a business crisis. It was a class of instruction. The *(Continued on page 92)*

(Continued on page 92)

41

A rare photograph of Dale Carnegie teaching the "breaking-through" class was published in *The American Magazine* in 1932. The basic Dale Carnegie Course, developed through trial and error, has undergone only a few modifications and remains essentially unchanged since its founder's death. Today, the class known as "coming out of your shell" occurs in the fifth session of the fourteen-week course. (Courtesy, *The American Magazine*)

Carnegie's marriage to Dorothy Vanderpool of Tulsa, Oklahoma, took place November 5, 1944, on the eighth anniversary of the publication of *How to Win Friends*. It was the second marriage for both of them. They met in 1942 when Carnegie was giving a lecture in Tulsa, and ten months later Dorothy moved to New York to become his secretary. An attractive, dynamic woman who listed "fencing" and "ballet dancing" among her hobbies, Dorothy in 1948 helped launch the Dorothy Carnegie Course in Personal Development for Women. (Courtesy, Wide World Photos)

Relishing his show-business contacts, the author of *How to Win Friends* was photographed in 1947 with film and rodeo star Gene Autry in one of New York's White Turkey restaurants. Carnegie, a former student at the American Academy of Dramatic Arts and road-show actor, made a brief Hollywood debut playing himself as a speech instructor in the movie *Jiggs and Maggie in Society*. (Courtesy, Wide World Photos)

In 1955, only months before his death, Dale Carnegie posed with one of his students (a personnel director at a Sherman hotel in Chicago) during the nationwide convention of representatives of the Dale Carnegie Institute of Effective Speaking and Human Relations. Dale Carnegie once told a friend that he read a little bit of his own book every day. By 1955 *How to Win Friends* had been translated into twenty languages, and today the Dale Carnegie courses are taught in more than sixty foreign countries. (Courtesy, Wide World Photos)

In September 1938, Carnegie was followed by wire-service photographers when he embarked on a vacation cruise. While royalties gave Carnegie greater freedom to travel and placed him much in demand as a public speaker, he continued to live modestly. "If I had all the money in the world, I couldn't wear more clothes," he told a reporter, "and I live exactly where I want to live." (Courtesy, Wide World Photos)

BUSINESS AND FRIENDSHIPS

Between 1912 and 1917, while Carnegie was getting his articles published, his public-speaking course was also beginning to prosper. His earnings rose to a handsome $500 a week. He began training assistants to teach the course. His expanding business brought him in contact with a growing number of interesting character types, ranging from rich industrialists to struggling young artists.

Carnegie developed three friends during this period who were particularly important to him. They were Homer Croy, Frank Bettger, and Lowell Thomas.

A precocious author from Carnegie's home town of Maryville, Homer Croy made a name for himself by selling an article to *Puck* magazine while still in grade school. Although he was five years older than Carnegie, the two boys probably got to know each other either in grade school or high school. Croy earned a place in Ripley's "Believe It or Not" by becoming the first student at the first school of journalism in the United States—the University of Missouri. He failed senior English, however, and never graduated.

Like Carnegie, Homer Croy found his way to New York, but by a different route. He worked as a reporter for the *St. Joseph Gazette*, *St. Joseph Press*, and *St. Louis Post-Dispatch*. Then he landed the plum position of assistant to Theodore Dreiser, editor of a number of magazines for Butterick Publications.

By 1914, Croy was an active part of a Greenwich Village circle in Manhattan. It met at the Liberal Club on MacDougal Street and included atheists, anarchists, dissidents, radicals, and free spirits. Among those who frequently crowded into Polly Holliday's smoke-filled cellar restaurant below the Liberal Club were journalists Max Eastman, Lincoln Steffens, and John Reed; novelist Sinclair Lewis; and the poet Louis Untermeyer.

Cleveland Rogers, an editorial writer and dramatic critic for the Brooklyn *Eagle*, recalled that Homer Croy "knew everybody" when he first came to Manhattan. It is likely that Croy introduced Carnegie to many of his Village friends. He also encouraged Carnegie's aspirations as a writer. Although Croy's life-style was far more bohemian than the earnest young Carnegie's, they came from the same roots. Both were struggling to make a name for themselves. Both began to see success at about the same time, Croy with his novels and Carnegie with his course in public speaking.

Carnegie dedicated *How to Win Friends* to Homer Croy, and they would remain lifelong friends. They often traveled together, and in later years Carnegie made it a habit to spend every Sunday with Croy. Even marriage would not change Carnegie's habit. His second wife says she "finally learned to plan my Sunday afternoons without him."

FRANK BETTGER

Another young man who was to figure prominently in Carnegie's life was Frank Bettger, a former third baseman for the St. Louis Cardinals who became an insurance salesman. After taking the course in Philadelphia, Bettger became an enthusiastic supporter of the Carnegie way.

In Bettger, Dale Carnegie saw elements of himself. Raised in poverty (his father died when he was young), Bettger had delivered papers and worked as a steamfitter's helper to aid his widowed mother. Becoming a baseball player had put him in center stage, but with his injury and early retirement from the game, Bettger had turned to selling and soon found himself down and out in a profession that seemed unsuitable for him.

For Bettger, as for Carnegie, the message of "act enthusiastic and you will be enthusiastic" gave him a new lease on life. Bettger was nothing less than a star pupil; he exemplified the Dale Carnegie course in action.

Years later, Dale Carnegie took Frank Bettger on a cross-country speaking tour sponsored by the United States Junior Chamber of Commerce. Carnegie and Bettger spoke four hours a night for five consecutive nights, splitting the program into segments of a half hour each.

Bettger's very popular book, *How I Raised Myself from Failure to Success in Selling*, was a testimonial to the Dale Carnegie techniques. Being touted by one of America's leading salesmen helped the Carnegie course. Carnegie also gained from Bettger's insights into salesmanship strategies. Carnegie would quote his friend at length in *How to Stop Worrying and Start Living*.

LOWELL THOMAS

By 1916, Carnegie had taken a permanent office in Carnegie Hall. This was about the time he began to replace the "Carnagey" spelling with "Carnegie." As he later told a reporter who asked him about the name change, "It was against my principles of showmanship to leave it the way it was." He attracted large audiences to introductory talks where he described the course and invited former graduates to speak. As a reporter for *Newsweek* later noted, "They came to scoff and stayed to pray." Enrollments grew steadily.

One of those attracted by the growing reputation of Dale Carnegie was a young speech teacher at Princeton University, Lowell Thomas. The meeting was fortuitous for both Thomas and Carnegie. In later years, a number of critics would remark how Dale Carnegie traded on the name of Lowell Thomas in selling his books and his programs. The fact is, Thomas and Carnegie had a friendship that was mutually rewarding in many ways.

Their earliest association occurred at a critical point in both their careers. At twenty-two, Lowell Thomas already held a master's degree from the University of Denver and a law degree from a Chicago night school (which he had earned while reporting for Chicago papers). In the Princeton area, Thomas was making some pocket money by giving illustrated talks to local clubs and societies on the subject of Alaska, which he had visited the previous summer.

Thomas visited Carnegie in New York because he needed assistance in preparing for an upcoming talk. Thomas had just been invited to deliver a lecture at the Smithsonian Institution in Washington, D.C., on the subject of Alaska. The Department of the Interior was conducting a See America First campaign. Secretary of the Interior Franklin K. Lane invited Thomas to present his illustrated lecture on Alaska to a number of congressmen. Although his speeches had made a hit in the local clubs, Thomas was wary of delivering the same presentation to a host of legislators at the Smithsonian:

> The first thing I did [Thomas recalled] was to head for New York in search of a public-speaking coach, someone who might help me shorten my talk. My guess was that I might be introduced at the end of a long roster of speakers—each extolling the glories of his home region— and in such a situation, brevity, wit, and eloquence could be golden assets. The man I found had a studio in Carnegie Hall, which was appropriate, as his name was Dale Carnegie.

On his side, Carnegie recalled his first meeting with Lowell Thomas: "I was immensely impressed, because that young man possessed just about everything necessary for success—an attractive personality, contagious enthusiasm, astonishing energy, and boundless ambition."

With guidance from Carnegie, Lowell Thomas's rambling three-hour speech was pared down to half an hour. It is unlikely that the two men had any differences about delivery style or content. During his days in law school, Lowell Thomas had advised his students to talk about their own experiences in their own words—advice that duplicated Dale Carnegie's public-speaking philosophy.

Feeling rehearsed and prepared, but still nervous about this once-in-a-lifetime opportunity, Thomas took the train to Washington. At the Smithsonian he was the last speaker on the agenda:

> Showing only my choice pictures, drawing on only the high spots from a talk I already had given more than a hundred times, I made my thirty minutes count. And when I was finished, I had them standing up to applaud. Instead

of a dragged-out afterthought to the conference, my part had been a sort of climax, and, afterward, governors and senators came up to shake my hand.

The coaching that Carnegie gave Thomas paid off handsomely. Thomas was recruited on the spot for the See America First campaign.

But the campaign never materialized. On April 6, 1917, the United States declared war on Germany. Secretary Lane invited Thomas to Washington and informed him the America First tour was canceled. Lane encouraged him, however, to travel to Europe with a cameraman to report on the war.

"This was how I became involved in World War I," Thomas later wrote. "This was what led to my experiences with all of the Allied armies from the North Sea to Arabia."

And, he might have added, all because of one successful speech. Just as Bettger showed what enthusiasm could do for a salesman, Thomas exemplified what public-speaking ability could do for a journalist. Launched by his speech at the Smithsonian Institution, Lowell Thomas would become the most recognized radio voice in the world. Every evening, in millions of American homes, families would gather around their radios for his nightly broadcasts.

WARTIME

World War I took Dale Carnegie and Lowell Thomas in opposite directions. On Tuesday, June 5, 1917, at the first blast of the factory whistles at 7:00 A.M., Registration Day began for 9,600,000 young men across America. Along with the rest, Dale Carnegie was handed a card to fill in with his name, address, physical characteristics, occupation, and a statement of willingness to serve in the army. By June 27, American troops had landed in France.

For Carnegie, war meant camp life in a hastily built barracks at Camp Upton, in Yaphank, Long Island. Constructing camps to house some 700,000 men called to active service was a monumental task. Camp Upton, like most camps, was only partially built by the time the recruits arrived. Draftees ready to fight for their country arrived in camp to find there weren't enough uniforms or rifles to go around. Many recruits drilled in their civilian clothes and carried wooden guns on parade. The facilities were so poor at the camp that a single hand pump was supposed to provide water for thousands of men.

Yet there were compensations. Camp Upton brought together the rich and the poor, the New York street kid and the Long Island estate owner. As one reporter observed, "The Bowery boy and the millionaire rub elbows, and the owners of Long Island showplaces sleep in cots next to their former gardeners."

Camp Upton also had the virtue of getting talent direct from New York stages. With songs composed by Private Irving Berlin, a camp show entitled *Yip, Yip Yaphank* was a rousing success that went on to Broadway. Irving Berlin's climactic number, "Oh How I Hate to Get Up in the Morning" ranked just behind "Over There" as the most popular song of World War I.

While Dale Carnegie was experiencing the life of a draftee in Camp Upton on Long Island, Lowell Thomas was tagging after General Sir Edmund H. H. Allenby and the British forces in Egypt. Before long, Thomas was pursuing a mysterious, blue-eyed Englishman who dressed in Arab robes, rode a camel, blew up train tracks, and made nighttime raids on the Turks—all on behalf of the Allied cause. This was T. E. Lawrence, whom Thomas would immortalize as the famed Lawrence of Arabia.

By November 7, 1918, the war was over. Along the front, as one general wrote, "The silence was stunning to ears attuned to the infernal roar." The number of Americans who had died in battle was 116,516. Endless parades welcomed home returning doughboys, but optimism gave way to cynicism and doubt. In the postwar economy, hundreds of thousands of returning soldiers faced unemployment and soaring costs of living.

Released from eighteen months of service, Carnegie relaunched his public-speaking courses at the YMCAs, but his business had lost ground during the war years. He almost had to begin the course from scratch. There was little interest from young men who needed to find employment before they could afford the fee of a public-speaking course.

WITH THOMAS IN LONDON

Once again, Lowell Thomas called on Carnegie for his services. When Thomas returned to New York City in 1919, he carried with him extensive film footage from his adventures and travels during the war in the Middle East. Thomas wanted Carnegie's help in preparing a script that would accompany the visual experience of sharing the front line with Allenby, Lawrence, and their men. Thomas ambitiously wanted to present an exciting, first-person lecture entitled "With Allenby in Palestine and Lawrence in Arabia." He would illustrate it with his vivid films of camel corps, Cairo, Jerusalem, Indian Lancers, and Bedouin irregulars. Although Thomas had ample material, he needed someone to help him pull it all together.

Thomas had already booked his first lecture in the Covent Garden Opera House in London. The opening was only two weeks away. Carnegie readily accepted the challenge. He was living in a rented cottage on Fire Island, and when Thomas's call went out, Carnegie packed in haste. When they arrived in London, Carnegie discovered that in the frenzy of packing, he had brought his bed sheets along with everything else.

During the voyage, Carnegie worked with Thomas and his cameraman to prepare the program. "All day and far into the night," Thomas recalled, "Dale, Chase [the cameraman], and I were huddled over our projector and scripts, working under the pressure of an opening less than two weeks off."

Carnegie was on hand for the first performance, but the best description comes from Gove Hambidge, a writer for *This Week* magazine:

> The royal Opera House, Covent Garden, London. A sixty-piece orchestra playing exotic Oriental airs. Out before the rich Oriental stage setting steps a dancer, twists her body

into strange postures. Offstage a voice softly intones the Mahometan call to prayer: La ilahu illa Allah! Allahu Akbar! A silver screen descends. Before it there walks a lithe, black-haired young man. . . .

Step by step he unfolds the strange drama of Lawrence's Arabian campaign . . . his words are timed perfectly to suit the action upon the screen. His deep, trained voice moves that audience now to bursts of laughter, now to sharp, emotional shocks.

Lowell Thomas's show was the surprise hit of the London season. The London opera season was postponed six weeks so Thomas could continue his show. It eventually moved on to capacity crowds at the Royal Albert Hall. "I saw London crowds stand in line for hours to buy tickets to hear him," Carnegie recalled. "That happened night after night, month after month."

Mission accomplished, Carnegie returned to New York. After some months of presenting the show by himself, Thomas cabled an offer to Carnegie to return to England and organize two road companies of the Allenby-Lawrence show. There was now demand for Lowell Thomas companies to travel through England, the U.S., and Canada. Thomas didn't want to do it himself, but he willingly made Carnegie his business manager for the traveling companies.

A TRAVELING SHOW

Carnegie was given the responsibility for hiring performers who would take Thomas's place on stage. Once the show was in Carnegie's hands, Thomas planned to travel to Australia with his wife Frances.

In the span of a few hectic days, Carnegie and Thomas pulled together all the props, costumes, and cast needed for two traveling companies. But as his ship pulled away from the London docks and Lowell Thomas waved farewell to his new business manager, he had a twinge of foreboding. "I remember thinking [Dale] looked a little overwhelmed by the rush of events."

His fears were well founded. When the boat docked in Melbourne, there was already a cable waiting for Lowell Thomas. The Allenby-Lawrence road campaign had folded. According to the cable, Dale Carnegie had suffered a nervous breakdown.

Although it is difficult, now, to figure out exactly what happened, Lowell Thomas's own interpretation may be the most accurate. According to Thomas, Carnegie had hired competent people and trained them well, but the show was so thoroughly identified with the personality of Lowell Thomas that it could not draw crowds without him.

The label of nervous breakdown may have exaggerated Carnegie's actual state of health, but the collapse of the show upset him. One reporter observed Carnegie when he was trying to present the show himself. At least once during the program, he lost his place in the script and attempted to ad lib. He startled the audience by saying, "Here is a beautiful picture of the East. Let us enjoy it in silence."

The task of running two road companies would have daunted even a skilled production manager. Moreover, not only did Lowell Thomas have the personality, voice, and presence to go along with the show, he also was intimately familiar with every scene portrayed in the films. He could ad lib at will. The show was, in effect, one of the earliest multimedia presentations. It was a kind of traveling Radio City Music Hall performance. No one but Lowell Thomas himself could maintain the multitude of effects.

"In the meantime," Thomas recalled, "we had lost a good deal of money and poor Dale was sick, blaming himself. There wasn't a thing in the world I could do about it at a range of 10,000 miles except to cable him my absolute confidence that he had done all anyone could expect."

Despite business woes, the friendship between the two men never flagged. In later years, Thomas again called on Carnegie to write a script to accompany some film of Sir Ross Smith, who had flown from England to Australia in twenty-eight days. In 1930, William S. Paley, the founder of the Columbia Broadcasting System, invited Lowell Thomas to host a weekly radio news show that was sponsored by a leading intellectual magazine of the day, *Literary Digest*. Thomas called upon Carnegie to work with Doubleday editor George Elliman and a manuscript reader named Ogden Nash, later famous as a humorous poet, to prepare scripts for the show.

Thomas wrote an introduction to the first edition of *How to Win Friends*, and his endorsements often appeared on advertising for Dale Carnegie's programs. When Thomas moved to his Hudson Valley estate in Pawling, New York, Carnegie was a frequent visitor. He played on Thomas's softball team known as the Nine Old Men, a team that included air ace Eddie Rickenbacker, boxing champions Gene Tunney and Jack Dempsey, and U. S. attorney Thomas E. Dewey, who would become governor of New York State.

When Lowell Thomas, Jr., was growing up in Pawling, he recalls a friendly, jolly man with gray hair and pale-rim glasses who often came to see his father on weekends. That jolly man was Dale Carnegie.

MARRIAGE AND A NOVEL

In 1921, Dale Carnegie married a woman from the French-German border area who claimed to be a countess. Her name was Lolita Baucaire. Little is known about how Carnegie met her. A first clue to her character is given by Carnegie's recollection of their wedding day: "I was married in a church in Europe; and the first words that my wife uttered after the ceremony were: 'Did you tip the janitor?'" The marriage was an unhappy one that ended ten years later. During the first two years of their marriage, they lived in Europe, while Carnegie worked hard to complete a novel entitled *The Blizzard*.

Writing was difficult for him. According to friends who later saw him at work, Carnegie would rewrite a passage as many as forty times and sometimes give up in despair. For a time, the Carnegies lived near Versailles. Although his surroundings were imposing, Carnegie was unimpressed. From Versailles he wrote, "Almost every day I spend an hour walking through what is probably the most famous park and garden in the world. Every

day I walk by the Grand Palace of the most ostentatious king
that ever misruled and oppressed humanity."

Carnegie claimed that Marie Antoinette's English Garden at
Versailles paled beside the natural splendors on the grassy banks
of the 102 River in Nodaway County, Missouri. Although on foreign soil, he was writing every day about his home town. He
imagined it vividly and with nostalgia. When the Maryville *Dem-
ocrat* requested an article from their far-flung correspondent,
Carnegie wrote on the vicissitudes of being a novelist.

> Since last January, I have been writing a novel about
> Nodaway and the 102 [River]. I have shucked corn down
> there by Bedison when the stalks were half blown down
> and covered with wet snow; I have milked and churned
> and cut wood when I wanted to go fishing; I have worked
> in the boiling sun until a sorrel mule would have fallen
> weak, spent, and exhausted if he had been trying to follow
> me; but all of these things all put together are just child's
> play in comparison to writing a novel. You won't believe
> this until you try it. Then you will say that I erred on the
> side of understatement. I am hammering away on this novel
> every day. . . .

There were interludes. Carnegie went wild-goose shooting in
the Hortobagy Desert in Hungary and planned to write an article
about the experience. Homer Croy, celebrating the publication
of his own fourth novel, *R.F.D. Number Three*, paid Carnegie a
visit in Versailles. The two friends drove 600 miles together
through the French countryside.

Carnegie praised Croy's new novel as "positively the best picture of farm life that has ever been written in the annals of
American literature." The visit inspired Carnegie to new exer-
tions.

The Blizzard, however, was a failure. Numerous publishers
rejected it, and Carnegie's literary agent told him the book was
worthless. In a blunt message, the agent informed Carnegie that
he was better giving up than continuing to try to write a novel,
since he plainly had no talent for fiction.

"I couldn't have been more stunned if he had hit me across the head with a club," Dale would later write. "I was stupefied. I realized that I was standing at the crossroads of life, and had to make a tremendous decision. What should I do? Which way should I turn?"

Putting the loss behind him, Carnegie returned to New York and began again teaching adult-education classes. Lolita Baucaire was still with him, and she made his life miserable. Whether or not she was actually a countess, she clung to the title as if it were her own. The farmboy manners of Dale Carnegie—though matured by years and experience—must have driven her near to frenzy.

By the end of the first year of their marriage, she realized that her American catch was neither an artistic novelist nor a wealthy businessman. Instead, she had married an enthusiastic idealist who labored over every word he wrote, suffered pangs of despair when his novel was turned down, and returned to what she saw as a prosaic future in public speaking.

Carnegie would later portray the rancor in their marriage in a biography of Lincoln that he considered his finest book. *Lincoln the Unknown* focuses on the relationship between Abraham Lincoln and his wife. The vehemence of Carnegie's unflattering portrait of Mary Todd reveals much about the mirror image of that woman, Lolita Baucaire:

> The Todds boasted of a genealogical chart extending back to the sixth century.... [Mary Todd] herself had been educated in a snobbish French school.... They had drilled Mary to speak French with a Parisian accent, and had taught her to dance the cotillion and the Circassian Circle as the silken courtiers had danced them at Versailles....
>
> Frequently, her anger was displayed by other means than words, and accounts of her violence are numerous and unimpeachable.... She led her husband a wild and merry dance, and she unchained the bitterness of a disappointed and outraged nature. She was always complaining, always criticizing her husband; nothing about him was ever right: He was stoop shouldered, he walked awkwardly and lifted

his feet straight up and down like an Indian. She complained that there was no spring to his step, no grace to his movements. She mimicked his gait and nagged at him to walk with his toes pointed down, as she had been taught at Madame Mentelle's.

Lolita Baucaire must have been shrewish indeed if she drove Dale Carnegie to divorcing her. Divorce was not a simple matter in 1931. Carnegie's religious values and midwestern upbringing preached against such drastic measures. His home life became unbearable, however. After exactly "ten years and forty days" Carnegie recorded, he and Lolita Baucaire parted ways.

In the meantime, he had begun to pull his teaching business together again. Rival teachers had begun using his methods and his textbook. Carnegie had to reestablish his name and reputation as the preeminent head of the genuine Dale Carnegie Course.

The YMCA once again became a home base for his classes, but he also made arrangements with the Brooklyn Chamber of Commerce to begin training New Yorkers on the other side of the river. Within a few years, business was flourishing. Carnegie scored a coup by being featured in Ripley's "Believe It Or Not" syndicated newspaper feature. Under a drawing of Carnegie, Ripley wrote:

Dale Carnegie has criticized 150,000 speeches or one speech a day for every day that has passed since Columbus discovered America. If all the men who have spoken before him had used only three minutes and had appeared before him in succession, it would have taken a solid year, listening day and night, to hear them all.

With his income restored, Carnegie bought a stucco house in Forest Hills, Queens. For a number of years after his divorce, he declined to reveal that he had ever been married. After the publication of *How to Win Friends*, he continued for a time to deny his marriage and divorce. The 1936 edition had a chapter on "Seven Rules for Making Your Home Life Happier," which later editions omitted. The rules ranged from "Don't, don't nag!!!" to "Read a good book on the sexual side of marriage."

Friends assured Carnegie that it was better for him to have been once married than a lifetime bachelor. By 1937 when he was interviewed by the *Saturday Evening Post*, Carnegie was finally willing to discuss his marriage with a reporter from the magazine. Among other things, he admitted to the reporter that *Lincoln the Unknown* was "strictly autobiographical."

PRIDE IN ACHIEVEMENTS

In the fourth session of the Dale Carnegie Course, the assigned subject for a talk is "an exhibit that represents an achievement." Students bring diplomas from little-known and renowned institutions. They bring plaques and trophies. A mother brings in a birth registration with her own thumbprint and the footprint of her baby boy. An engineer with graying hair holds up a report card with his A in calculus—the final hurdle in getting his master's degree in engineering. A young man brings a photograph of his grandmother at the Copley Hotel in Boston, where he took her for a special night out. There is a blue ribbon from a horse show; a medal won by a javelin thrower; a golfer's nine iron; a framed portrait of a cigarette that is broken in two ("I finally gave it up!"). A sales brochure. A tee-shirt. A letter of congratulations.

Andy is thirty-two years old, an intense-looking man with black hair, bushy eyebrows, and deep-set eyes. He is financial officer at a regional bank. Although always dressed in a dark gray suit, his clothes seem somewhat sloppy and uncomfortable, as if his jacket could slide off his shoulders at any moment. His voice is low-pitched, nasal. His hand gestures—when he attempts them—are highly artificial. He has such an air of serious concern that it borders on gloom. That aura, however, works in his favor when he is talking about something he believes in or urgently wants to communicate to people in the room.

Andy's "exhibit that represents an achievement" is a wedding ring that he slips off his left hand and holds up for the class to see.

When I was in college, my social life wasn't so good. I didn't date very much. I never went out very much. I used to hang around with my friends, but I didn't get to know many women. After I graduated and started working, my social life didn't get any better. I kept wondering, "When is it going to get better?" and I didn't know.

One night, I went to a place near my office for a few drinks. Some people were dancing. I noticed this woman come in, and she looked very attractive, but I didn't say anything. I found out later that she noticed me, too, right away. But that was later.

Anyway, she came over to me and asked whether I wanted to dance. I don't dance very well, so I said, "No." (Laughter from the class. Andy smiles.) Then I asked her if she wanted a drink, and *she* said, "No." (More laughter.) So I didn't want to dance, and she didn't want to drink, but somehow we got started talking about something.

So anyway, then we started going out, and about a year later we got married. I'm very happily married. For me that was a very big thing, to meet a woman like that—because I never thought I would. That's why this ring is important to me.

SUCCESS IN A COURSE

With the disastrous reception of *The Blizzard* and the end of his marriage, Dale Carnegie, now well into his thirties, had few achievements of which he could be proud. Yet he derived much pleasure from the demonstrations of achievements large and small which the students of the Dale Carnegie Course in Public Speaking displayed. For some of those students, the diploma, the ribbon, or the letter of thanks signified a high point in their lives. Showing it off, hearing the round of applause, they began to place greater value on their accomplishments.

As always, Carnegie gloried in the changes reflected in their faces and their attitudes when these students earned recognition for their achievements. He felt a teacher's pride when the students who took the Dale Carnegie Course became shining examples of success. Although he didn't have the novelist's talent of Homer Croy, the salesmanship of Frank Bettger, or the speaking ability of Lowell Thomas, he learned from each of them. And whatever he learned, he passed along to his students.

His writing failed. His marriage failed. His salesmanship was often wanting. But his course in public speaking remained the jewel in his crown, his one major achievement.

The rewards the course brought him were as numerous as the students who learned a simple lesson from session four—that their achievements counted for something.

CHAPTER 9

A BEST-SELLER THE AUTHOR DIDN'T WANT TO PUBLISH

I N JANUARY OF 1931, THE YEAR DALE CARNEGIE DI-
vorced Lolita Baucaire, New York City had 82
breadlines serving 85,000 meals a day. Even those who still held
on to their jobs felt the pinch of the Depression. The stock market
crash had wiped out the savings of many families. Layoffs and
plant closings threatened employees everywhere.

No longer buoyed by financial optimism, some people saw the
crash as a sign of a social injustice. There were still millions of
Americans, however, who continued to believe that they would
succeed through individualism, hard work, and personal
achievement.

This was the audience, in the throes of the Depression, that
welcomed *How to Win Friends and Influence People*.

RECOVERY, CARNEGIE STYLE

Carnegie claimed that he, like many others, lost most of his savings in the stock market crash of 1929. Given his habit of listening to friends and enthusiastically pursuing new opportunities, it seems he followed the path of so many small investors, hurling everything into the investment wave that finally broke in the fall of that year.

When the stock market collapsed on October 29, 1929, William C. Durant, the founder of General Motors Corporation, made a quick calculation. His imagery would have appealed to Dale Carnegie. Durant reckoned the losses on Wall Street in silver dollars. Placed one on top of another, all those dollars would stand 100,000 miles high.

Despite his losses, Carnegie was one of the lucky ones. In the following three years, he managed to hold on to his modest house at 27 Wendover Road in Forest Hills, as he began reorganizing and conducting his classes in New York City. While unemployment continued to climb (an estimated 3,200,000 men were out of work by April, 1930) and the breadlines grew longer, his courses had greater appeal than ever to those who desperately wanted to find jobs, hold on to jobs, or improve their incomes. By the spring of 1932 Carnegie had once again established his program, and he had some small savings. With no classes until the fall and the summer hours heavy on his hands, he decided to take a trip to China.

Despite the escape—he was to call that trip to China "my greatest adventure in living"—the images of the Depression lingered with him as he made his way to Shanghai. There he witnessed a poverty more pervasive than anything imagined in America. Noting that "about two million Chinese die each year from floods, pestilence, and starvation," Carnegie saw the hunger and starvation that surrounded him. As his ship pulled into the harbor, sampans swarmed beneath the ship's rail. The Chinese boatmen held out nets to catch slop from the ship's kitchen. On the streets of Peking, he saw a girl "picking up and eating watermelon seeds that a man spat on the dirty sidewalk as he ate."

As always, Carnegie drew lessons from the sights that he witnessed. This lesson was a personal one. Compared to the Chinese, Carnegie counted himself fortunate. Even at his worst moments, he had many ways to earn a living. The vision of China's terrible, age-long struggle with suffering and poverty certainly made his own struggle with occasional setbacks seem trivial by comparison.

"Suppose my classes did fail and I had to go back to milking cows?" he mused. "It would be a veritable Vale of Kashmir in comparison to the poverty, disease, and misery that 400,000,000 Chinese were enduring in the Orient."

Far from failing, however, his courses prospered during the fall and winter of 1932. Carnegie continued to expand his enterprises.

Carnegie had by now settled on the two-minute talk as the ideal requirement for each speaker. But what was the right format for a talk? Carnegie claimed that he consulted with many of his instructors, who were on the faculties of speech departments, or active in business administration, advertising, and promotion, before settling on the ideal format for a speech. This format he called the Magic Formula. Used to this day, the Magic Formula consists of an *example*; followed by a specific, clear-cut *point*; and concluding with a *benefit*—the reward to be gained. "This is a formula," Carnegie concluded, "suited to our swift-paced way of life."

The text of the Dale Carnegie Course was the result of evolution. At first, Carnegie simply posted rules or points on a series of postcards he distributed to instructors. The postcards evolved into a series of booklets given both to instructors and to students taking the course.

In later years, Dale Carnegie would claim that *How to Win Friends* was the direct offspring of these booklets. Adding information gathered by hired researchers, he said, he simply assembled the booklets under one cover and made them coherent for a popular audience. Behind the evolution of the book is a slightly different story, however. It was the strength of the course itself, rather than the strength of Dale Carnegie's writing, that spawned one of America's best-selling books.

LEON SHIMKIN

By 1934, Dale Carnegie had published four books of his own, in addition to the book that he had written with J. Berg Esenwein in 1915. *Public Speaking; A Practical Course for Business Men* was brought out in 1926 by Association Press, the publishing arm of the YMCA. When Carnegie began reorganizing his classes in the early 1930s, he reissued the same book as *Public Speaking and Influencing Men in Business* in 1931.

Lincoln the Unknown was published by Century in 1932. The obscure publishing house of Greenberg brought out *Little Known Facts About Well Known People*, two years later. For *Little Known Facts*, Carnegie had hired researchers to find out facts about prominent men. After selecting his candidates for the book, Carnegie interviewed many of them and collected the sketches in a single volume.

Carnegie had submitted both *Lincoln the Unknown* and *Little Known Facts About Well Known People* to Simon & Schuster, a New York publishing house barely ten years old that had launched itself with a line of crossword puzzle books. (Its most popular nonfiction book at that time was *The Story of Philosophy* by Will Durant, a big best-seller derived from a series of lectures that were given by the author.) An editor at Simon & Schuster turned down both of Dale Carnegie's first books.

In 1934, the business affairs of the company were in the hands of an energetic, diminutive young man by the name of Leon Shimkin. Although not yet a principal in the company, Shimkin had already gained the nickname "Little Golden Nugget" for his sound business judgment. Simon & Schuster was fast becoming an important publishing house, and Leon Shimkin was working hard to keep up with the business end of it. Shimkin did not interfere in editorial matters. Dale Carnegie, however, was an exception.

Shimkin had just bought a house in Larchmont, in Westchester

County, about twenty miles from New York. One evening, he accepted the invitation of a neighbor to attend a lecture by Dale Carnegie. The lecture turned out to be a promotion for the course. After a brief introduction, Carnegie introduced a number of businessmen who had taken the course. He asked each, in his own words, to tell how the course had benefited him.

> I was particularly impressed with Carnegie's technique [Shimkin recalled], avoiding any great display of oratory, but in simple terms showing the effectiveness of his course from the mouths of satisfied customers. . . . I had no idea of taking a course in public speaking when I came to the house that night, but the effect of the speeches on me was to make me feel that I could do better than the men who spoke that night, and I enrolled for the course.

The class of about thirty met once a week at the Hommock Country Club. The group included some lawyers, one assistant district attorney, an executive of A&P, an inventor who headed a condenser company, a realtor, and a financial investor accompanied by his wife, who had been active in Westchester social service work. Despite their professional credentials, many of the speakers were shy. Shimkin noticed how Carnegie gradually got them to speak out "with enthusiasm and spirit."

The eleventh session was what Carnegie called the "WIR" (Welcoming in Response) talk. In his memoirs, Shimkin recalled:

> I was completely fascinated by this talk. [Carnegie] talked about how to come to grips with an adversary who disagreed with you completely. His technique called for finding something that the other man felt that you could agree with, and making it clear that you agreed with him on that point completely, and little by little the other fellow would concede a point in your favor until you found yourself together agreeing with each other more than disagreeing. . . . His basic approach was that by looking for the good and the positive, you would create an atmosphere attractive to the

other person and would be most likely to receive a response of a similar nature.

That evening I felt that Mr. Carnegie had outlined the technique of making friends and influencing people.

Inspired by what he heard that night, Shimkin promptly wrote a manuscript report to the editors of Simon & Schuster. He proposed a book written by Dale Carnegie called *The Art of Getting Along With People*. Max Schuster, head of the editorial department, suggested that Shimkin present the idea at the next editorial board meeting.

In the nineteen thirties, it was a tradition for Dale Carnegie course members to eat together during the first part of each session. At the next dinner, Shimkin sounded out his neighbors on their reaction to the course. Each commented on how he or she had tried using the Dale Carnegie approach with secretaries, partners, colleagues, business associates. They all agreed on one thing: the principles worked.

That evening after the session, Shimkin approached Carnegie with the suggestion that he write a book.

"What publishing house do you represent?" Carnegie asked.

"Simon and Schuster."

"I won't submit another book to Simon and Schuster," Carnegie declared. "Your editors turned down my first two manuscripts, and they won't get any more. Besides, I don't have time to work on a new book right now."

Shimkin persisted. He explained that editors have different reactions to different manuscripts. If the book was based on the down-to-earth, specific techniques that had received such warm approval from the class, Shimkin was sure it would succeed.

Then he proposed a course of action. If Carnegie would say where he was going to deliver his next "WIR" lecture, Shimkin would have a stenographer on hand to take it down.

"It's your money. You're free to spend it," Carnegie responded.

Shimkin made certain there was a stenographer at the next "WIR," which was being held at a Dale Carnegie session on Long Island. The report was typed up and sent to Carnegie. A few days later Shimkin received a call. Carnegie thought the talk read well as transcribed, and he wanted to proceed.

Carnegie's secretary, Vera Stiles, had helped assemble the manuscript for *Little Known Facts About Well Known People*. Shimkin suggested that he work personally with Stiles to assemble a preliminary manuscript, using files of letters from previous students along with copies of his speeches. First draft in hand, Carnegie would then add or rewrite material to achieve the final form.

The act of writing was always painful for Carnegie. He was never able to work swiftly, even with material that he knew cold. At his English Tudor house on Wendover Road, he would rise early and fling on his battered tweed hat and jacket for an early morning walk. After an 8:00 A.M. breakfast, he retired to his third-floor office. There he took up his writing labors in a big easy chair, with a yellow pad perched on his knee. When he was suffering from writer's block, he sometimes rewrote the same paragraph dozens of times before giving up in frustration.

When the season and weather permitted, he occasionally went into the garden to plant spring bulbs. A secretary who worked for him in later years recalled that Carnegie "said it was a good way for him to break writer's block. I found that he did this often and it satisfied something deep inside him. He would come back to work renewed."

After two years, Dale Carnegie submitted the completed manuscript to the editorial committee of Simon & Schuster. The committee approved it, and Carnegie signed a contract for a book called *How to Win Friends and Influence People*.

PUBLICATION

The first edition of *How to Win Friends*, published in November 1936, had an introduction entitled "A Short-Cut to Distinction" by Lowell Thomas. The introduction begins with a vivid portrayal of thousands of eager participants thronging into the grand ballroom of the Hotel Pennsylvania in New York to hear Dale Carnegie speak. It concludes with the encomium, "Dale Carnegie, by helping business men and women to develop their latent possibilities, has created one of the most significant movements in adult education."

The ten-page introduction (included at the end of hardcover and paperback editions published today) encapsulates the entire Dale Carnegie rags-to-riches story. Noted Thomas: "Dale Carnegie's own career, filled with sharp contrasts, is a striking example of what a man can accomplish when he is obsessed with an original idea and afire with enthusiasm." Coming from the foremost broadcaster in America—from a voice heard nightly in almost every household that owned a radio—this was an auspicious endorsement for Carnegie's book.

Beyond that, Leon Shimkin had a promotional idea that turned out to be an inspiration. To promote the book effectively, he decided Simon & Schuster should send a copy to 500 graduates of the Dale Carnegie Course. An accompanying letter from Shimkin himself pointed out, from one graduate to another, "the book would be helpful in refreshing us on Mr. Carnegie's principles." Incidentally, Shimkin noted, the recipients of the book should consider passing it around to their office or sales staffs, who might also benefit from Dale Carnegie's principles. The letter to 500 graduates brought orders for 5,000 copies. Simon & Schuster had to increase the original print order of 1,200 immediately.

Shimkin then ran a full-page ad in *The New York Times*, quoting John D. Rockefeller and Andrew Carnegie on the virtues of getting along with people. Again, the book went back on press.

Carnegie began presenting a copy of his book to each member of his classes. Soon *How to Win Friends and Influence People* was selling 5,000 copies a week. By the end of 1936, it was on *The New York Times* best-seller list, where it remained for the next two years.

Earning royalties of twenty-five cents a copy, Carnegie made $150,000 in the first twelve months of publication. He was much in demand for lectures and radio shows. The book caught the eye of Charles Vincent McAdam of the McNaught Syndicate who immediately called up Carnegie and said, "I read your book and I wonder if you'd write a newspaper column for me."

Carnegie's reply: "I'd love to write one. Come on over to my house tomorrow night and have dinner."

Within two hours, McAdam had a verbal agreement from Carnegie to write the columns. The result of that dinner was a series of "Capsule Preachments" that ran in seventy-one newspapers across the country.

During the same dinner, McAdam had the temerity to ask, "By the way, Mr. Carnegie, where is Mrs. Carnegie?"

Carnegie replied, "Oh, hell, we couldn't get along; we got divorced."

As book sales boomed, so did the popularity of the course. Carnegie gave his program a formal name, The Carnegie Institute for Effective Speaking and Human Relations, and appointed class directors from his alumni. As the program expanded, he selected and trained area managers who would conduct classes throughout the United States—and eventually in more than sixty countries throughout the world.

In the midst of the Depression, Dale Carnegie was fast becoming a millionaire.

A BEST-SELLER

Becoming an immensely successful author shocked Carnegie.

"When I was writing this book," he later mused, "I hoped that it might sell 15,000 or 20,000 copies. I was astonished to see it crawl up to the best-seller class."

He was very pleased when his publisher announced that the sales of *How to Win Friends* were second only to the Bible. Occasionally, Carnegie used this line himself when trying to sell another book or article. Yet the enormity of those numbers left him somewhat bewildered.

Being in the limelight also made him even more self-conscious about his own shortcomings. He discovered that best-selling authors were expected to *be* what they preached. No matter how often he protested that he had no special powers, the public now saw him as the man who could "win friends and influence people."

The following year found him writing, with considerable signs of frustration, to the editor of his hometown paper:

> I realize now that healthy people don't write books on health. It is the sick person who becomes interested in health. And, in the same way, people who have a natural gift for diplomacy don't write books on *How To Win Friends and Influence People*. The reason I wrote the book was because I have blundered so often myself, that I began to study the subject for the good of my own soul.
>
> You will probably recall one of the rules in the book says not to argue. Well, I was always arguing.

Toward Leon Shimkin, Carnegie showed only his gratitude. When Shimkin sent Carnegie the 100,000th copy of his book, Carnegie returned it with the inscription, "Every morning I arise and face the East and thank Allah that you came into my life." Even Shimkin seemed somewhat overwhelmed by the unexpected (though pleasurable) success of *How to Win Friends*. When the book hit the quarter-million mark, he wrote to Carnegie (in a letter dated March 12, 1937):

> Dear Dale:
>
> If one year ago a friend of mine were to have told me that today I was going to send an author the 250,000th copy of his book I would have either referred him to the nearest psychiatrist or to Robert Ripley for the believe-it-or-not cartoon. Yet, believe it or not, I am sending you under separate cover the 250,000th copy of *How to Win Friends and Influence People*.
>
> I hope to be able to repeat this very pleasurable experience for the 500,000th copy and also for the 1,000,000th copy.
>
> Beyond that, reason totters.
>
> Sincerely,
> Leon Shimkin
> SIMON & SCHUSTER

INFLUENCING PEOPLE

On May 6, 1935, President Franklin D. Roosevelt issued an executive order establishing the Works Progress Administration, which would remain in existence for the next eight years and two months. The National Industrial Conference Board calculated that 9,711,000 were unemployed, about triple the number at the beginning of the Depression.

In 1936, the year *How to Win Friends and Influence People* appeared, Sinclair Lewis's chilling novel *It Can't Happen Here* became a play that opened simultaneously in 21 theaters in 17 states, drawing more than 250,000 spectators. It would run for 260 weeks. People sang "Brother, Can You Spare a Dime?" "Smoke Gets in Your Eyes," and "Ten Cents a Dance." On their radios they listened to Fanny Brice as Baby Snooks, Edgar Bergen and Charlie McCarthy, and Bing Crosby performing with Bob Burns on the *Kraft Music Hall* program. In 1936 they were still reading Hervey Allen's picaresque novel, *Anthony Adverse*, along with the newly published *In Dubious Battle* by John Steinbeck and Margaret Mitchell's *Gone With the Wind*.

William Randolph Hearst paid $6,000 a day to maintain his estate at San Simeon, California; J. P. Morgan was getting ready to launch his fourth yacht; and Rockefeller Center was rapidly nearing completion.

Published in this climate of Depression-conscious, entertainment-hungry, rags-and-riches America, what was the overwhelming appeal of *How to Win Friends and Influence People*? What nuggets of wisdom and inspiration did it contain that would make Dale Carnegie a household word in a nation crippled by economic hard times? And why should thousands of readers today continue to buy and read a best-seller published in 1936?

Nothing is more difficult to predict than what will make an overnight best-seller—and nothing is easier to explain in retrospect. Since the day it appeared, however, publishers have been intrigued (and critics of Dale Carnegie offended) by the staying power of these 200-plus pages chock full of common sense, homespun wisdom, optimistic resolutions, quotations, platitudes, and aphorisms. A quick glance at the pages reveals what intrigues some as well as what offends others. What gives the book its staying power, however, has more to do with American culture than with the contents of the book.

From the very first page, Dale Carnegie sets a tone of warmth and intimacy with the reader.

"As I look back now across the years," he confesses in the preface, "I am appalled at my own frequent lack of finesse and understanding. How I wish a book such as this had been placed in my hands twenty years ago! What a priceless boon it would have been!"

These three sentences were probably the most effective advertising copy ever written for a book. In a few words, author Dale Carnegie admits his own shortcomings, gives the reader a moment to identify with the wishes of a younger man, and extols the benefits ("a priceless boon!") of the book the reader now holds in his hands.

He then embraces the largest possible audience: "Dealing with people is probably the biggest problem you face, especially if you are a business man. Yes, and that is also true if you are a housewife, architect, or engineer."

The end of the preface makes the strongest case for reading the book:

> If by the time you have finished reading the first three chapters of this book—if you aren't then a little better equipped to meet life's situations, then I shall consider this book to be a total failure, so far as you are concerned. For "*the great aim of education*," said Herbert Spencer, "*is not knowledge but action*."
>
> And this is an *action* book.

The italics are Carnegie's. By calling it an "action book," he was inadvertently creating a whole new category in publishing —the now familiar self-help book. Practically every self-help book published since *How to Win Friends* has borrowed either form, style, or substance from this path-breaking best-seller that established the genre.

In this respect, *How to Win Friends* was a book without precedent. Carnegie did not write his book for anyone to read passively. The intention of the book was at one with the intention of the course: to bring about a change in the attitude or behavior of the reader.

To this end, Carnegie included a nine-point section on "How to Get the Most Out of This Book." Among other suggestions, he urged his audience to read each chapter twice, underlining important phrases, and to review it at least once a month. Carnegie also suggested that each reader ask someone to check up weekly on his or her progress in applying the principles. Far-fetched as this sounds, Carnegie was serious. This was not a book to stand idle on the bookshelf. It was a book to *use*.

Carnegie regarded his courses as a "laboratory in human relations." *How to Win Friends*, therefore, was a compendium of laboratory results. "This book wasn't written in the usual sense of the word," he informed his readers. "It grew as a child grows. It grew and developed out of that laboratory, out of the experiences of thousands of adults."

Throughout *How to Win Friends*, Carnegie relied heavily on quotations from famous industrialists and financiers, including the Rockefellers, senior and junior, J. P. Morgan, Henry Ford, the publishing magnate Cyrus H. K. Curtis, and Andrew Carnegie. He borrowed freely from men of wisdom, including Confucius, Lao-Tse, Croesus, Benjamin Franklin, Jesus Christ, and Marcus Tullius Cicero. His authorities included scientists (Luther Burbank, Albert Einstein), musicians (Toscanini, Chaliapin), authors (Turgenev, Dickens), philosophers (William James, Immanuel Kant), performers (Eddie Cantor, Bing Crosby), politicians (Roosevelt, LaGuardia), royalty (Duke of Windsor, Prince von Bulow), inventors (George Eastman, Harvey Firestone), and many little-known entrepreneurs, salesmen, and businessmen.

The net effect of all this name dropping was not lost upon the public. The Depression had created an "us" and "them" mentality that was pervasive. Those caught in the downward spiral of financial collapse felt cheated, deprived, their livings torn from their hands through no fault of their own. On the other side of the economic line were the rich few who seemed completely unscathed by economic hard times. The have-nots standing in breadlines could see the haves pass by in limousines. Those who were still employed but caught in the steady grind could observe wealthy employers, politicians, entertainers, bankers, and financiers who escaped the imprisonment of economic necessity.

What set the haves apart? What special skill did the privileged have that was unavailable to those caught in the daily grind? Dale Carnegie said it was the ability to get along with people and to get things done that set some apart from others. He quoted at length and presented many examples to substantiate this observation. Then, with the principles at the core of the book, he told his audience how they could *take action* to escape the rank-and-file.

By emulating the human-relations skills of those who had succeeded in the past, Carnegie said, his readers would also succeed. Such skills were within reach of everyone!

WINNING FRIENDS

The book served another Depression-era need that had more to do with temperament than with economics. Times were hard. People felt bad. Unemployed men returning home to face the bewildered faces of their children could no longer say where the next day's meal would come from. The provider could no longer provide. And that hurt.

Being willing to work hard wasn't enough: Work itself was unavailable. Even the employed wage-earner felt the deprivation. Worst of all, he felt the blow to his self-esteem.

The stress on the family was intense. Tempers flared. Poverty did not draw families together; it split them apart. Husbands and wives felt the strain. They struggled to maintain a precarious balance until things got better—and prayed that they *would* get better.

Into this world of frayed nerves came a book entitled *How to Win Friends and Influence People*. There was actually little in the book about close friendships, but much about getting along with people, avoiding arguments, defusing explosive situations. "Show respect for the other man's opinions," Carnegie suggested. "Never tell a man he is wrong." "Begin in a friendly way." "Get the other person saying 'Yes, yes' immediately." And: "If you are wrong, admit it quickly and emphatically."

Carnegie also described how to get other people to see and do things your way, but with minimal conflict. "Don't criticize," cautions Carnegie. "Call attention to people's mistakes indirectly," and "Let the other fellow feel that the idea is his."

To the critics of Dale Carnegie, there was a certain quaint naivete—and, what seemed worse, an element of toadying—in these principles of compliant behavior. Carnegie never vented his anger toward the system, and this lack of spleen vexed his critics. For them, the task of social observers was to show that the system was to blame for what had happened.

Although Carnegie preached getting along with people, it was clear that the industrialists who ruled the system did not worry about the niceties of getting along with their fellow men. Men such as John D. Rockefeller and Andrew Carnegie were not likely to admit that they were wrong, or to "show respect for the other man's opinions." They ruled by economic intimidation and brute force. They survived quite nicely while others suffered.

Among intellectuals, labor, and even the middle class caught in the Depression, there was ample anger toward the ruling class. Despite their anger, many Americans felt it was unlikely the system would change. In a Depression-weary country, most did not want revenge; they just wanted to get along.

And something was wrong with the way they were living. The weight of necessity was crushing kindness, consideration, and simple graces. With homilies like "Don't criticize, condemn or complain" (principle two) and "Smile" (principle three), Carnegie in effect restored a moral balance to an intensely demoralized public.

Carnegie was a sentimentalist. That, too, was appealing. Kindness, sympathy, tolerance, and understanding are qualities the book espoused. Approvingly, he quoted Elbert Hubbard, urging his readers to put this earlier writer's "sage advice" into action:

> Whenever you go out of doors, draw the chin in, carry the crown of the head high, and fill the lungs to the utmost; drink in the sunshine; greet your friends with a smile, and put soul into every handclasp. Do not fear being misunderstood and do not waste a minute thinking about your enemies.

Companionship, family love, domestic peace, and greater understanding among friends and coworkers—these were the causes that Dale Carnegie supported. Social change was far from his mind.

The book struck a chord. People felt better for having read it. Whether or not they underlined passages, reread it monthly, or applied the principles as Carnegie wished, they recognized the good intentions of the author. The heady sprinkling of names of the rich and famous, the wise and the learned, made Carnegie's readers feel as if they were hearing lessons from a man (a *Carnegie*, no less!) who was worldly-wise in his associations and learned in his judgments. At the same time, the warm, humble tone of Carnegie's prose told his reading audience that here was a common man who just wanted answers to the profound puzzle of how their world worked.

The Depression had smashed the machine of living. With the principles of *How to Win Friends*, Dale Carnegie, for many, began to fix it again.

PARODY AND CRITICISM

Subjecting *How to Win Friends* to close critical scrutiny is a little like asking a puppy dog to explain why he's loved. The critics had a heyday with it. They deplored not only the prose and sentiments, but also the general tenor of the reading public who bought the book.

A parody appeared within a year, entitled *How to Lose Friends and Alienate People: A Burlesque,* by Irving D. Tressler. In his introduction, Tressler suggests the way to get the most out of this book: "You must have a deep, driving desire to want to make others dislike you just as much as you dislike them, a vigorous determination to recognize that most people are about as interesting as a semiannual report of the U.S. Gypsum Co."

Tressler's book parries, one-for-one, the conciliatory strategies of *How to Win Friends* in chapters that include "How to Make a Poor First Impression," "How to Discourage Overnight Guests," and "Always Turn a Conversation Into an Argument." Tressler complained that Carnegie was inciting people to be boring:

> This book [wrote Tressler in his parody] is the outgrowth of years of experience in being bored. It is the product of the experiences of dozens of friends in being bored. It is the result of being the victim of thousands of statements commencing: "We know you're terribly busy, so we're only staying a minute—!"

More serious writers had more serious complaints, although almost invariably they resorted to sarcasm rather than direct attack. James Thurber led off with a review that appeared in the *Saturday Review* in January, 1937. Thurber made sardonic comments about Carnegie's wisdom and concluded:

> Mr. Carnegie loudly protests that one can be sincere and at the same time versed in the tricks of influencing people. Unfortunately, the disingenuities in his set of rules and in his case histories stand out like ghosts at a banquet.

The following month, a *New York Times* reviewer deplored the implication that Dale Carnegie's principles would give the reader a "shortcut to distinction." The same reviewer, however, gave his readers some aphoristic advice of his own:

> By all means let us follow the sensible advice so cheerfully offered in Mr. Carnegie's pages. And at the same time let

us try to keep our balance and clarity of thought. You cannot gather grapes from thorns or figs from thistles; and there is no royal road to any kind of success or happiness. But improvement in tact and imagination may indeed make us more efficient and more agreeable. And a genuine understanding of our fellows is a thing worth working for, for its own sake.

Sinclair Lewis waited almost a year—until *How to Win Friends* had sold its 600,000th copy—before launching his attack by reviewing nine examples from the book. "These nine illustrations of principle, out of hundreds in the book," Lewis concluded, "ought alone to enable any student to make more money, though there is the slight trouble that they may make it difficult for the student himself, and impossible for his wife, to live with him." Carnegie's mission, as Lewis perceived it, was to "make Big Business safe for God, and vice versa."

Poor reviews could not slow the pace of sales. By 1937, the very phrase "win friends and influence people" had become so bandied about in the popular press, at cocktail parties, and in society high and low, that it was simply a part of the language. A number of cartoonists poked fun at the book. In the September 1937 issue of *Esquire*, a voluptuous woman in the monthly pinup illustration was shown reposing in a scant negligee, reading *How to Win Friends*. More serious criticism came from journalists and intellectuals who saw the book as a distinct sign of the decline of public taste.

An official biographer of Carnegie, William Longgood, portrayed the author as being "the target of mass abuse and ridicule" after *How to Win Friends* appeared. When the Dutch Treat Club of New York invited Carnegie to speak, a member of his staff advised against it. The club included editors, publishers, and advertising men—savvy, cynical, and hard-bitten. Carnegie's advisor cautioned him, "They're the toughest bunch in America. They'll eat you alive."

Carnegie accepted the invitation, however, and disarmed his critics in his opening remarks:

I know there's considerable criticism of my book. People say I'm not profound and there's nothing in it new to psychology and human relations. This is true. Gentlemen, I've never claimed to have a new idea. Of course I deal with the obvious. I present, reiterate, and glorify the obvious—because the obvious is what people need to be told. The greatest need of people is to know how to deal with other people. This should come naturally to them, but it doesn't.

I am told that you are a hostile audience. But I plead "not guilty." The ideas I stand for are not mine. I borrowed them from Socrates, I swiped them from Chesterfield, I stole them from Jesus, and I put them in a book. If you don't like their rules, whose would you use? I'll be glad to listen.

According to Longgood, Carnegie received a thunderous ovation.

There were few men or women whom Dale Carnegie could not win over, once he was in their presence. But there was an unwritten chapter to *How to Win Friends and Influence People*. Carnegie realized there were some people for whom none of the rules applied. It was impossible, under any circumstances, to get along with them. The unwritten chapter was to deal with those times when "somebody has to go to jail, be spanked, divorced, knocked down, sued in court."

Carnegie later said that he never wrote the chapter because he had an opportunity to take a vacation in Europe before he could complete it. Thus he had to send the book to the publisher without his final word on human relations. Given the difficulty of reconciling such a chapter with the rest of the book, the vacation was probably the better course of action.

POSITIVE REINFORCEMENT

Today, *How to Win Friends and Influence People* has gone through hundreds of editions and several revisions and updates. More than 15 million copies are in print. It is assigned reading for participants in the Dale Carnegie Course in Effective Speaking and Human Relations.

At session seven, midway through the course, the class divides into small groups. Five or six students sit in a circle facing each other. In one group at a recent session:

Ben. A chisel-featured, stern-looking man in his early sixties; he is the owner of a real estate and construction business.

Shawn. A young, red-haired woman who is a sales representative for a large computer company.

Rich. A stocky black man in an open-collar shirt; he is a foreman at a local tool and die shop.

Frank. A twenty-four-year-old single man with the build of a football player; he is a CPA with one of the Big Eight accounting firms.

Kathy. A thin woman in her late twenties; a graphics designer and the mother of a two-year-old.

The instructor leads the entire class in a warm-up, then gives instructions for Part A of session seven. Each group then begins. In this one, Ben turns to Shawn: "Shawn, you have a very nice smile," he says, looking her straight in the eye.

"Thank you," she says.

Rich is next. "Shawn, I remember the first time I came to class," he says. "You were very helpful, and you asked me a lot of questions. I think you're interested in people, and I like your curiosity."

"Thank you."

Frank says, "Shawn, I've seen you gain a lot of confidence since the first class. You seem very motivated and I know you're going to succeed."

"Thank you."

"Shawn, you are very warm and outgoing, and it always makes me feel good to see your enthusiasm."

"Thank you."

Rich is the next subject. Shawn tells him that she appreciates his sense of humor. Ben brings up something that Rich said in a previous talk—how he bailed himself out of a difficult situation. He says this is a good example of Rich's ingenuity. Kathy says she has noticed that he seems much less intimidated than he was when he first got up to speak.

Before the end of the first part of session seven, each person will have heard about qualities that others in the group find appealing or attractive. There is no criticism.

It is a formal, round-robin exercise in positive reinforcement —a live demonstration of principle two: "Give honest and sincere appreciation," and principle six: "Make the other person feel important—and do it sincerely."

The set-up is as contrived as a laboratory experiment. The members of the group previously have met together only six times. Some have not even spoken to each other directly before now. Yet, as the compliments go around and around the circle, it quickly becomes apparent that the actual insights and perceptions matter far less than the attempt to reach across the circle and try to offer honest and sincere appreciation. There is a heartfelt effort to make each person feel important.

The outcome of the experiment? Perhaps a single word that rings true, perhaps a quality noted for the first time. Some reassurance that someone is improving, being heard, earning recognition.

For every person it is different, of course. In the supportive atmosphere of this Carnegie-created course, one thing is certain: no one is worse off from the experiment.

The method is simple. The results are almost predictable. Listening to the comments of one person praising another, one after the other, all around the room, students gradually notice how rarely direct words of praise are voiced, anywhere, at any time.

In the safety of this laboratory of human behavior, students are trying an experiment run in thousands of classrooms for over seventy-five years. If the experiment works, their self-esteem gains something. Even if they doubt the sincerity of those who praise them, they may hear single phrases that they believe.

As Dale Carnegie tried to explain in *How to Win Friends*, the experiments are ridiculously simple. The results have been casually noted for thousands of years. And the complexities of dealing with human nature continue to work, as they have always worked, in the most mundane ways.

AN ACTION BOOK

In the years since *How to Win Friends* appeared, Dale Carnegie has been portrayed many times as the apostle of the easy road to success. His critics believe he led millions down a path to materialism.

Dale Carnegie simply took it for granted that greater financial success was a worthy goal. Many of the anecdotes he related in *How to Win Friends* demonstrated how human relations principles could lead to higher incomes. Bethlehem Steel president Charles Schwab earned a million dollars a year because he was good at handling people. A coal salesman opened a tough account after years of failure because he became interested in a buyer's concerns. A businessman saved himself thousands of dollars by *not* telling a customer he was wrong.

Carnegie used money as one yardstick of success, but he was as content to use friendship, peace of mind, freedom from worry, or any other yardstick that came to hand. His point was that certain actions brought certain results. One way to show those results was in terms of career success. Nevertheless, making money and getting ahead did not exclude other forms of reward.

His example of a stockbroker is typical. In *How to Win Friends*, Carnegie describes a stockbroker who changed his life by starting to smile at people at home and at the office. The broker concludes that "smiles are bringing me dollars, many dollars every day." Carnegie went on to say that wearing a smile also changed the way the stockbroker dealt with people. The broker felt as if he had revolutionized his life—that he was "richer in friendships and happiness—the only things that matter much after all."

Carnegie cited evidence that supported his point, but he rarely dictated to the reader "this is what you must do." So he did not chart a path to a certain future. Like the Dale Carnegie Course, the Dale Carnegie book offered a variety of benefits, including increased self-confidence, improved human-relations skills, and more pleasure out of life. It was up to the class member or reader, not Dale Carnegie, to choose a personal goal.

Ever the pragmatist, Carnegie had seen his techniques work for thousands of famous and not so famous individuals who had used them to accomplish their own goals. These tools he offered to millions of readers who eagerly picked them up. *How to Win Friends*, as Carnegie stated clearly in the introduction, was an *action book*. How his readers chose to act with the tools he provided was their own business.

To this day, every edition of *How to Win Friends and Influence People* has the ending that Dale Carnegie intended—two blank pages with the heading "My Experiences in Applying the Principles Taught in This Book." Thus, the book is to be completed in real life, by the reader.

Although mocked by the critics, Carnegie earnestly hoped that his laboratory of human relations would always be open to the ideas, the applications, and the experiences of his readers. The publication of *How to Win Friends and Influence People* opened the laboratory for everyone.

CHAPTER 10

PASSING
THE TORCH

T HE FIRST ROYALTY CHECK FOR HOW TO WIN FRIENDS was a staggering $90,000. That is the equivalent of over $700,000 in late-1980s dollars. That much money could easily have purchased half a dozen or more homes such as the stucco one Dale Carnegie owned in Forest Hills, Queens.

For a week, the check lay on his desk. Then his secretary asked him, "Don't you think it should be deposited?" Carnegie answered, "It has come too late for them to see it, but wouldn't my mother and father be proud of it?"

He deposited the check knowing his life would never again be the same.

Although riches did not change his life-style, the mantle of fame did. Up to the book's publication, the Dale Carnegie Course was essentially a one-man operation averaging less than a thousand students a year. In a short time, twenty times that number were enrolled. Even today, a significant number of enrollees say they are signing up because they have read the book.

In 1937, while the critics were still taking pot shots at his prose, Carnegie started an advertising campaign in *The New York Times*. A banner headline promised:

INCREASE YOUR INCOME
SPEAK EFFECTIVELY

The ad offered a free demonstration at the Hotel Astor by Dale Carnegie, "author of *How to Win Friends and Influence People* ... the fastest selling book in America. No other nonfiction book in the history of the publishing business has ever sold so many copies in such short a time."

The ad pictured Carnegie, who left college before graduating, over a caption of four somewhat mystifying degrees: B.Pd., B.C.S., F.R.G.S., and Litt. D. The meaning of these were, respectively: Bachelor of Pedagogy, Bachelor of Commercial Science, Fellow of the Royal Geographical Society, and Doctor of Humane Letters. The doctorate was an honorary degree Carnegie received in 1936 from the Maryland College for Women.

The ad also pictured Lowell Thomas. He endorsed the course as "unique; a striking combination of public speaking, salesmanship, human relations and applied psychology—a course that is as real as the measles and twice as much fun."

The ad boldly promised fifteen benefits of the course. Among other things, participants would learn to think on their feet; increase their income; win more friends; get to know intimately forty ambitious men and women; and develop their latent powers and improve their personalities.

The ad detailed how the course worked. In 1937, there were sixteen regular sessions (today there are fourteen). Private dining rooms of hotels and restaurants were the classrooms, and the first part of each session was at dinner. There were also nine Tuesday night lectures on topics such as improving your memory and developing your personality. The list of organizations that had offered the course ranged from New York Telephone to the Junior League. The Dale Carnegie Institute of Effective Speaking and Human Relations would send two booklets to those who could not attend. One listed the names and addresses of 520 men who had recently completed the course. They were willing to give references. The other booklet outlined the course.

The topical Tuesday night lectures drew huge audiences to hear Carnegie speak. The crowds were so large that eventually the Hotel Astor declined to host the mass meetings because they strained the hotel's facilities. The surge in popularity put a strain on Carnegie as well. After he wrote the book, it was difficult for him to resume his normal, offstage manner after a talk. People expected him to be equally dynamic in private conversation. They expected him to be a charismatic and fearless leader beloved by all.

Anyone would have found it difficult to live up to the myth. This Missouri farmboy found it almost impossible. Once off the stage, he was quiet and reserved. No master of the interpersonal skills he taught, Carnegie frequently forgot people's names and occasionally became argumentative.

He tried to avoid the limelight. He would repeatedly switch tables in restaurants to avoid fans. He told a colleague who helped shield him from the public and screened personal invitations:

> Harold, I wish you would avoid, whenever possible, relaying these invitations to me and here is why. Before I wrote the book *How to Win Friends*, people did not seek my company. I was just Dale Carnegie, teacher of adult education classes, and in no way sought after. Now that I have written the book and it has had such a phenomenal sale, people expect me to be something "out of this world," someone different. But when strangers meet me and begin to get acquainted, they find I am just like their next-door neighbor, that I am not someone with a dynamic personality. Then they feel let down. I sense that feeling and then I am embarrassed. That is why I always avoid, whenever possible, the invitations of strangers.

Avoiding invitations didn't sufficiently protect his privacy. So at the height of the popularity of *How to Win Friends*, he went to Europe. Without him, the Carnegie Institute of Effective Speaking and Human Relations foundered. In 1939, he had to return home to rescue his business. A few months earlier, Carnegie had been cheerfully advising the public to face the Depression with a positive attitude. Now he had to deal with its realities himself. He let go the staff of thirty-five, closed the 42nd Street office in Manhattan, and moved the operation to his Forest Hills home.

The World War II years were difficult ones because both instructors and students were scarce. Carnegie continued the radio broadcasts he had begun back in 1933 on the Maltex Hour. Starting in 1943, he was broadcasting every Thursday night over the Mutual Network. Called "Little Known Facts About Well Known People," the show grew out of his 1934 book of the same name.

Two events in 1944 dramatically affected the remaining eleven years of his life. He married for the second time and set up a national organization for his courses.

DOROTHY

Dorothy Vanderpool of Tulsa had a connection with Dale Carnegie that antedated meeting him. In 1941, she had taken the Carnegie course from H. Everett Pope, the proprietor of the Oklahoma School of Business, Accountancy, Law, and Finance.

In 1939, Pope had written Carnegie telling him that he had been reading excerpts of *How to Win Friends* to some of his graduates. It helped them find jobs. Carnegie wrote back that Pope had no right to teach the Dale Carnegie Course. Pope then went to New York and struck a deal with Carnegie to let Pope's school officially offer the course. Pope thus became the first of many business-school sponsors of the course.

Carnegie met Dorothy Vanderpool after giving a speech in Tulsa. He had lunch with her, her mother, and Everett Pope. He corresponded with her after the visit. In October, 1943, he proposed that she come to New York as his secretary. The working relationship/courtship was stormy. She once quit after an argument, but Carnegie persuaded her to stay.

They married on November 5, 1944, the eighth anniversary of the publication of *How to Win Friends*. The wedding at the Boston Avenue Methodist Church in Tulsa was small. Only members of her family and a small group of friends were present. Before the ceremony, Dale Carnegie said to Everett Pope, "If they play 'People Will Say We're in Love,' I'll just cry." They did play the song, but he stayed dry-eyed. Said one friend later, "He was so excited about marrying Dorothy that he never even heard the song."

After the ceremony, Carnegie declared: "Even after I wrote that book, it took me eight years to influence a woman to marry me."

LICENSING

A month before their marriage, Carnegie had set up the network of licensees that remains the foundation of the business today. In 1945, Carnegie created the privately held company, Dale Carnegie & Associates, that continues to own the business. He was president, and Dorothy was vice president. Today, Dorothy is chairman of the board. Her son-in-law from her first marriage, J. Oliver Crom, is president.

In the same year that he married, Carnegie began publishing pamphlets on controlling worry for use in the course. After four years, he put them in book form. With only a bit over 6 million copies sold, *How to Stop Worrying and Start Living* has never achieved the immense success of *How to Win Friends*.

Yet the *Worry* book is one of the better selling books of the twentieth century. In 1948 it was the second best-selling nonfiction book of the year, just behind Dwight D. Eisenhower's *Crusade in Europe* and just ahead of Alfred Kinsey's *Sexual Behavior in the Human Male*.

Despite its author's track record, the publication of the *Worry* book received little attention. The daily *New York Times* ignored it. The Sunday *Times* said:

Mr. Carnegie's latest blueprint for a social Garden of Eden is so choked with formula, exhortation, and case history that no reader will go entirely unrewarded.

Time magazine was more enthusiastic. They predicted that it "was likely to make a best-selling bang that will surprise even its sophisticated publishers."

Carnegie stuck to the formula that had worked so well in *How to Win Friends*. He filled the *Worry* book with anecdote after anecdote showing how the famous and not famous controlled their worry:

- Booth Tarkington had believed he could face anything in life except blindness. Then, in his sixties, he went blind and discovered he could accept it.
- Montaigne, the French philosopher, learned: "My life has been full of terrible misfortunes—most of which never happened."
- Earl P. Haney of 52 Wedgemere Avenue, Winchester, Massachusetts, thought his ulcers were going to kill him. So he decided to make the most of the time he thought he had left. He bought himself a coffin and a cruise ticket around the world. En route, he stopped worrying, gained ninety pounds, and as soon as he got home went back to business.
- Ora Snyder, a homemaker of Maywood, Illinois, had to earn money when her husband fell ill. She had only ten cents' worth of ingredients. Unworried, she made candy out of egg white and sugar to sell to schoolchildren. "During the first week, she not only made a profit of $4.15, but ... put a new zest into living."
- Then there was a Tulsa stenographer who had the dull job of filling out printed forms for oil leases for the Gulf Oil Corporation. Resisting "the fatigue that is spawned by boredom," she made a contest out of trying to improve her productivity. The result was more energy and more vitality. That stenographer,

Carnegie notes in his book, ended up marrying Dale Carnegie.

The *Reader's Digest* created two articles from the *Worry* book in 1948 and 1949. The message of the first article was "Live in day-tight compartments," a restatement of the saying "Don't cry over spilt milk." The second focused on irrepressible spirit—the mark of a man. Emulate the tire in meeting the shocks of the road, Carnegie advised. Be flexible.

By 1948, the course was being offered in 168 cities in the United States and Canada. And Dorothy Carnegie was beginning to get more involved in the business. She says it was out of boredom.

One evening when the Carnegies were on vacation in the Canadian Rockies, Dorothy told her husband she wanted to dance. He wanted to go to bed early. To keep her occupied, he suggested that she write a course for women. The result was the Dorothy Carnegie Course in Personal Development for Women.

Her course, she later said, was not "just another charm course for women. We try to encourage women to enlarge their mental horizons. We look upon the training somewhat as a kind of 'old age insurance.'" Although Dorothy worked for twenty years to establish the course, it never made money. In the late 1960s, she killed it. "We're not philanthropists here, darn it," she told a reporter. "We're in business to make a profit."

The course may have failed, but it did lead to her first book. The Greystone Press published *How to Help Your Husband Get Ahead in His Social and Business Life*, by Mrs. Dale Carnegie, in 1953. She followed her husband's example and combined anecdotes from course participants with the experience of notables. She even used a number of the anecdotes Dale had been using in his books and speeches.

Like Dale, Dorothy emphasized the importance of enthusiasm. Both quoted Frederick Williamson, one-time president of the New York Central Railroad, who declared that enthusiasm is the secret of success in business. Ralph Waldo Emerson was cited: "Nothing great was ever achieved without enthusiasm." And both husband and wife devoted pages to Frank Bettger and his formulation: "Act enthusiastic and you'll be enthusiastic."

Both authors also quoted Sir Edward Appleton, who won the Nobel Prize in Physics. "I rate enthusiasm," said Appleton, "ahead of professional skills as a recipe for success in scientific research."

Dorothy Carnegie emulated her husband's predilection for interim summaries. She would summarize each part by providing the reader with short, aphoristic principles. She even adopted her husband's practice of including the street address of class members she cited. The technique supposedly added verisimilitude.

Time was one of the handful of publications that reviewed *How to Help Your Husband Get Ahead*. It predicted that she had almost surely written a best-seller.

Time was wrong, although the book did provide ample material for pithy magazine articles. It was condensed in *Coronet* magazine, and was the basis of an article in *Better Homes and Gardens* in which Dorothy Carnegie summed up her advice in ten rules:

1. Develop courage, self-confidence, and poise.
2. Express yourself effectively—at home, in your social life, and in any civic or business activity.
3. Perfect your grooming and also your appearance.
4. Increase your conversational ability.
5. Broaden your interests and develop your personality.
6. Remember names and faces and other people's interests.
7. Put in nine full innings of making your home life happy.
8. Try to get along better with others and win more friends—for yourself and your husband.
9. Raise your standard of loving; don't be the girl he left behind him.
10. And the most important of all: *Be enthusiastic*. There is positively no substitute, no facsimile, for enthusiasm.

Dorothy Carnegie wrote a second book in 1958 called *Don't Grow Old—Grow Up*. An explicit attempt to carry on the Carnegie philosophy, *Don't Grow Old* emphasizes the benefits of a change in attitude. Don't worry about staying young, she advised. Focus on the growth and wisdom that are the rewards of maturity. Her second book is still in print. Three copies are given as prizes in session ten of the Carnegie course. The class votes for the three members who give the most effective talks on "How To Control Worry and Reduce Tension."

The Carnegies had their only child together in 1951. Dale was in his sixties when Donna Dale Carnegie was born. Norman Vincent Peale remembers Dale walking into Marble Collegiate Church and saying to him, "Congratulate me! My wife just had a baby—and I'm sixty-three years old!"

When Donna was a toddler, he would take her for walks by the pool at the Forest Hills house. Often, he would begin talking to someone enthusiastically and forget he was babysitting. When he returned to the house, Dorothy would ask, "Where's Donna?" He would have forgotten all about her. Eventually, he filled in the pool and planted a rose garden to make sure Donna wouldn't fall in while he was talking to someone.

Donna has only what she calls fuzzy memories of her father. She remembers scenes from a trip to Bermuda shortly before he died. She also recalls taking walks with him to his office and on his Belton, Missouri farm.

After World War II, Dale had bought a 1,250-acre farm in Belton, where his parents had moved from Warrensburg. He had 850 head of Brangus cattle, a combination of Brahman and Angus breeds. He would visit the farm every two or three months for a week or so. His second cousin, Russ Wernex, who managed the farm for him, remembers that Dale loved the outdoors. He liked riding horses and was interested in conservation. He planted hedges to protect the land. Neighbors such as J. Weldon Jackson remember Carnegie as gracious and friendly. He enjoyed sitting around, visiting with people over a Coke.

Dorothy sold the farm after Dale died and raised Donna back east. A graduate of Macalester College in St. Paul, Minnesota, Donna Dale Carnegie now raises horses in Lake Oswego, Oregon. She has no official involvement with the Dale Carnegie Institute.

THE HONORARY DEGREE

Dale Carnegie's social status never came close to equaling his fame. The year he died, however, he received an honorary degree from his alma mater. As *Newsweek* pointed out, it was the first degree he had ever received from what was now called Central Missouri State College at Warrensburg. It was also the first honorary degree Central Missouri had ever awarded.

The ceremony was a bittersweet occasion. A colleague said the degree wouldn't have pleased him more had it come from Harvard or Oxford. The sadness was that in the summer of 1955, Carnegie's health was beginning to fail. He took his own advice: it's only the prepared speaker that deserves to be confident. After several weeks of preparation, however, he found himself unable to remember his speech. For over forty years Carnegie had taught many thousands of people to speak from the heart. Free yourself from a manuscript, he urged. A written speech "will keep you from speaking naturally and with sparkle." Now he had to read his speech.

His theme was a familiar one. He told the summer session graduates about the magic of enthusiasm, the real measure of a man's success in life. He also recalled his own college days. He had had trouble with Latin. "No," he said, "I didn't quite graduate, and I'm glad I've forgotten everything connected with Latin. Learning isn't so important, it's what kind of a man you make out of yourself while you're learning that counts."

Despite his having to read it, the talk went well. The *Newsweek* reporter commented:

> He spoke with his usual firmness (and enthusiasm), in an accent still of the Midwest. His natural body gestures were

well timed, and his persuasive content was high. No doubt
only the dignity of the occasion restrained his listeners from
encouraging shouts of "Atta boy!"

Three months later, on Tuesday, November 1, 1955, he was
dead of what was then diagnosed as uremia, a blood disease.
Since then, Dorothy has speculated that his real affliction was
arteriosclerosis or hardening of the arteries, which was commonly misdiagnosed thirty years ago. The funeral was November
third at the Church in the Gardens in Forest Hills. He was buried
in the Carnegie family grave in Belton, Missouri. A marble slab
covers the grave, and a small marker reads: Dale Carnegie,
1888–1955.

AFTER CARNEGIE

The press paid little attention to his death. *Time* and *Newsweek*
both printed brief notices. His obituary in *The New York Times*
filled a column. The immense success of *How to Win Friends*
was the focal point of the obituaries. There was no recognition
of the size of the adult-education program he started.

Partly by chance, partly from a desire to keep a low profile,
the Carnegie course at the time of Carnegie's death had a surprisingly private aura for such a public program.

The organization was persistent in keeping alive the image of
its founder through advertising and continual self-promotion.
Carnegie himself had performed a kind of public service for his
graduates, but the organization he left behind was intensely
private. With Dorothy Carnegie as chairman of the board, it has
remained to this day a closely held, family business.

From the media coverage in 1955, few would have realized
that the Dale Carnegie Course was the largest adult-education
course in the country. To insiders, on the other hand, it was a
bit like religion. The fervor was epitomized in the Dale Carnegie
Club International, the Carnegians, founded in 1949. This quasi-
independent alumni organization sought to keep the spirit of

the course alive after graduation. By the early 1950s, there were 264 local clubs with over 8,500 members. There was even a Dale Carnegie song praising "the man who gave us inspiration. . . . We're never in a hurry, we've lost the art of worry. We will always sing the Carnegie song."

The Dale Carnegie Club declined in the sixties despite substantial growth in course enrollments. From the fifties to the mid-eighties, the enrollments increased in the face of negligible public awareness. In 1955, when Dorothy took over the business there were about 55,000 enrollments annually. By the mid-1970s annual enrollments had reached 80,000. In 1988, they exceeded 150,000.

Not until the mid-eighties, however, did public awareness start to catch up with the import of a $100 million educational enterprise. A breakthrough came when Lee Iacocca published his autobiography. He credited the course with changing him from a shrinking violet into a leader equipped to rescue the multibillion dollar Chrysler Corporation. Millions of people read that Iacocca had sent dozens of introverted employees to the Dale Carnegie Course at the company's expense. This testimonial led thousands of people to enroll.

The surge in business led Carnegie management to become more relaxed about publicity. Since the book *Iacocca*, there have been major articles in *The Wall Street Journal* and *The New York Times* and a report on ABC's "20–20." Even *Smithsonian* magazine published a comprehensive report on the course and the man.

The publicity has been predominantly positive. The "20–20" segment, for instance, was so enthusiastic that the weeks after its airing saw a large surge in business. Reporters have a tendency to highlight the exuberance of the Carnegie approach: "Thunderous applause and chants of 'Go! Go! Go!' " "Enthusiastic approval, warm as mother's milk, is the dominant emotion." "Session fourteen of the Dale course gets off to a raucous start as a roomful of men and women jump up, sit down, crouch, and stand up again while chanting a standard Carnegie warm-up:

> The Grand Old Duke of York,
> He had 10,000 men.
> He marched them up the hill;
> He marched them down again.

To reporters who invariably observe just a couple of sessions, the raucousness of the course is its most salient characteristic. Since they don't witness the changes in class members over fourteen sessions, reporters almost universally discount the testimonials that the course changed a class member's life. To the reporter from *Smithsonian*, for example, course graduates "seem content simply to have a new bag of tricks."

The basic thrust of the publicity is positive enough to leave Dale Carnegie & Associates pleased. It makes easier the process of spreading the word. The fundamental reason for their optimism for the business has nothing to do with the publicity or even their belief in the positive attitudes the course teaches. It is mathematics.

The course has always depended on word of mouth. More graduates mean more referrals. The number of graduates now exceeds three million, and the number of new referrals increases each year. Thus the potential for enrollments grows rapidly.

In the first quarter-century of the course, there were 20,000 graduates. In the second quarter-century, about one million. And in the third quarter-century, about two million. At the current rate, the torch that Dale Carnegie lit will pass to over four million in the next twenty-five years.

CHAPTER 11

THE POWER

OF THE GROUP

NOT LONG AGO, ONE CARNEGIE COURSE STUDENT told how he rehearsed for a speech at a trade show:

> I was standing in front of my mirror trying out the speech.
> I was comfortable with the material, but felt very strange to
> be looking at my reflection. Then I tried recording my voice
> as I rehearsed. The playback sounded even stranger than
> my reflection looked. When I prevailed on my spouse to
> listen to a run through, it still felt strange. The day of the
> trade show came. After I gave my talk, my only sensation
> was one of relief and a feeling of stiffness in my hands. I
> realized that came from tightly gripping the lectern. I saw

that practicing by myself—or even with one other person —was no practice at all for the real experience.

The number of students who made similar statements to Dale Carnegie made him realize the power of the group. The group experience gave an advantage to course participants when they stood up to meet the challenge of speaking before an audience. Carnegie never explicitly tried to understand the dynamics of groups and the psychological dimensions of what was going on in his classes. Nonetheless, he made the group instrumental in affecting behavioral change in class members.

His course has never been one of group therapy, but the parallels between group therapy and the Carnegie course are very strong. Their connections are somewhat surprising. Group therapy was not widely used or recognized until after World War II, when the Carnegie course was over thirty years old.

In an in-depth review of what makes group therapy work, psychologist Irwin Yalom identified ten factors, virtually all of which are present in the Carnegie course:

1. *Imparting information—therapists or group members communicating instructions or advice.* In the course, the instructor and graduate assistants, former class members, relate the information. Carnegie's most noted books (*How to Win Friends*, *How to Stop Worrying*, and *The Quick and Easy Way to Effective Speaking*) are the textbooks. Consequently, there is a strong sense that the information is coming straight from an almost mythical Dale Carnegie himself.

2. *The instillation of hope, especially as members of the group see progress made by the others in the group.* In every Carnegie session, a class member observes the performance of every other class member and witnesses the growth. Although class members are often slow to see change in themselves, they can't help noticing changes in their fellow class members.

Take, for example, the change in Kathy Thornton, a recent class member. In session one, Kathy was terrified. Her instructor had to lead her by the hand from her seat to the front of the class so she could introduce herself to the class. By session four, she was able to relate an absorbing story. She had almost died in a car crash when she was a high-school senior because she let her date drive after having had too much to drink. Witnessing such a change makes class members feel there is some power to this experience.

3. *Universality, or the recognition that others share your concerns and worries.* In the introductory session, everyone shares their reasons for enrolling. As Frank Ashby, Vice President for Instruction of Dale Carnegie & Associates, says, "People come in feeling they're atypical. They find out through the course that they're not alone."

4. *Altruism, or the feeling that you're being helpful to or are needed by other group members.* Applause is voluntary and spontaneous, but everyone in class knows that he is helping others—and being helped himself—by the applause that begins and ends every talk. There's a shared awareness that this process works because it's a group effort. No one is giving talks to mirrors or studying a book in isolation.

5. *The corrective recapitulation of the primary family group.* In other words, *the feeling of being part of a group which is similar in some ways to the structure of a family.* Just as a group leader has parental overtones, an instructor often functions as a parent directing the family's activities.

6. *The development of socializing techniques—or the ability to improve interpersonal skills through interaction.* The interaction reaches a focus in the middle of the course when class members give and receive compliments to and from one another.

7. *Imitative behavior—the opportunity to model your behavior on the appropriate behavior of others in the group.* After each talk, the instructor reinforces behavior by commenting positively on an aspect of the talk. The goal is to bring that appropriate behavior to the attention of the class as well as the individual who just spoke.

8. *Interpersonal learning—the opportunity to test a variety of behaviors with others.* The Carnegie classroom is a place where people feel it's all right to fail. Class members feel comfortable trying out new techniques of dealing with people both inside and outside the classroom. There is no negative feedback in the course. So, getting lost in your talk, running out of time, pacing

back and forth, having your voice crack, feeling that your heart is beating so loudly that someone in the next room can hear it —none of these problems matters. And when you see someone else overcome them, it gives you the courage to try.

9. *Group cohesiveness—the feeling of belonging to an appealing group.* After a few weeks of giving talks in which most class members reveal much about themselves—key life experiences, hopes, disappointments, accomplishments—class members feel that this group, which began as a gathering of strangers, has become a special collection of people. After giving talks on worry and emotion in sessions ten and thirteen, many class members will confess to having shared experiences that they had never told anyone. Others will comment that the session felt like going through group therapy.

10. *Catharsis—the opportunity to release feelings in a safe environment.* Whether it's showing anger and excitement or acting out the role of a surly bartender or a grizzled prospector, class members show feelings in a way that many say they haven't done since childhood.

Dale Carnegie was not a psychologist. But he didn't need to be. For the most part class members are not dealing with deep-seated psychological problems or concerns. They are typically trying to shake a fear of public speaking or improve their management skills. When they see progress in the area of life they came to change, they're usually satisfied, especially since most people find that the fourteen sessions give them benefits beyond what they anticipated.

Carnegie saw that the process of improvement in speaking made people receptive to all sorts of other learning. He used that receptivity as the foundation for a program where developing interpersonal skills and developing a positive, less worried outlook became the bulk of the curriculum. He saw that class members who had gone through the public-speaking portion of the course and were feeling part of the group were likely to accept the human-relations portion, even if that hadn't been their intention.

During the fourteen sessions, the Carnegie course becomes a comfortable environment. There is lots of positive reinforcement and a strong sense of community. At the end, however, there is a strong push to get class members *out* of that environment and into the real world again. Instructors will sometimes end the fourteenth session with the exhortation that the course is actually beginning, not ending, for now comes the chance to put these newfound skills to work in the real world.

LIFE BY THE RULES

If the course has been a success, a class member graduates feeling that he or she has internalized a new set of principles. The graduate now has rules for dealing with people, setting goals, reducing worry, improving memory, and keeping a positive attitude. Typical is the report that a forty-five-year-old accountant gave to his class:

> I was just about to give her a piece of my mind, when I pictured Dale Carnegie sitting on my shoulder. He was saying to me, "Now, wait a second, maybe there's a different way to handle this situation." So, I thought for a second about what I might do. I remembered some of the human-relations principles. First, about how the only way to win an argument is to avoid one. And then I thought about his principle of showing respect for the other person's ideas.
>
> So instead of yelling at my secretary Sarah because the report wasn't ready, I asked her what the problem was. Then I listened as she described a series of problems getting the copier fixed that she couldn't have anticipated. And then I listened as she suggested a way we could get the report done—by her staying late! Not only did we not argue, but the report did get out on time.

This report of the application of Dale Carnegie's human-relations rules is typical in two regards. That pause to think before speaking reflects a consciousness of Dale Carnegie that comes through the fourteen sessions. And familiarity with the easily memorized principles makes it easy to remember which one applies to a particular situation.

In common with many religions, self-help groups, and even businesses, the Dale Carnegie Course provides a set of rules for living: Encounter a problem, review the possible solutions, and then apply the appropriate ones. Very early in the course, every class member receives the aptly titled *Golden Book*. This palm-sized, eight-page booklet contains thirty human-relations principles and thirty worry principles. They distill essentially all the advice that Carnegie provides in *How to Win Friends* and *How to Stop Worrying*.

Dale Carnegie was far from the first to try and codify rules for living. Benjamin Franklin was one of Carnegie's favorite examples; he quoted Franklin eleven times in the two books. Franklin's maxims in *Poor Richard's Almanac*, which he masterfully compiled as *The Way to Wealth*, set a strong example for Carnegie. There Carnegie saw the advantages of the well-turned phrase and the succinct expression. Where Franklin was asking his readers to improve and motivate themselves ("Women and Wine, Game and Deceit/Make the Wealth small, and the Wants great"; "He that lives upon hope will die fasting"), Carnegie's inspiration was to use the same techniques directed toward interpersonal behavior.

How did Carnegie come up with his rules? In 1930, six years before *How to Win Friends* appeared, a psychologist and a writer joined forces on *Strategy in Handling People* to illustrate "psychological principles with incidents from the careers of successful men." The authors, E.T. Webb and J.J.B. Morgan, related many of the same anecdotes that Carnegie used six years later. From the *Strategy* book, Carnegie borrowed an example of Benjamin Franklin learning to avoid direct contradiction and becoming more persuasive. Like the earlier authors, Carnegie describes Dean Donham of the Harvard Business School "walking the sidewalk in front of a man's office for two hours rather than stepping into his office without a perfectly clear idea of what I am going to say and what he—from my knowledge of his interests and motives—is likely to answer." Carnegie liked the anecdote so much he repeated it, the second time in italics.

Carnegie also discusses John D. Rockefeller's managerial acumen. Carnegie, like the earlier authors, admired Rockefeller for being able to praise sincerely a subordinate who lost a million of Rockefeller's dollars in South America.

Both books were covering the same ground and harvesting similar material. One received little notice; the other became one of the best-selling books of all time. The difference? Carnegie's ability to extract a pithy lesson from an anecdote and phrase it memorably. Where Webb and Morgan suggest: "To win the other fellow's liking and cooperation, remember that his personal interests are different from your own," Carnegie says: "Talk in terms of the other person's interests." Webb and Morgan advise: "The first step in persuading people to act as you wish, is to present your plans in such a way as to get a 'Yes Response' at the very start. Throughout your interview, but above all at the beginning of it, try to get as many 'Yesses' as you possibly can." Carnegie, by contrast, takes eight words, not fifty-one, to exhort his readers to action: "Get the other person saying 'yes, yes' immediately."

SELF-HELP GROUPS

What happens in the Dale Carnegie course, however, is much closer to what observers of self-help groups such as Alcoholics Anonymous (AA) view as the acceptance of a specific ideology. In AA, the guidelines include "Easy does it," "A day at a time," "But for the grace of God. . . ."

Alcoholics Anonymous was founded in the mid-1930s. There is no evidence that its founder, Bill W., or any of the other early leaders of AA had any knowledge of Dale Carnegie's efforts. Dale Carnegie may have been a pioneer in using groups as a means to change people's behavior, but because his efforts were commercial and outside any academic or intellectual school, he didn't develop followers. Carnegie may have been first, but those who followed, whether as professional or lay leaders of self-help and therapeutic groups, had to make their own discoveries.

In AA, Weightwatchers, and the Dale Carnegie Course, the sharing of experiences is an important part of the transfer of ideology. Not only are the teachings in easy-to-remember form, but the accompanying stories emphasize the principles. In the Carnegie course, there are a series of commitments to practice the human relations and worry principles. Progress reports follow these commitments. The reports have punch lines that are typically a restatement of the principles. The shared experiences indoctrinate both speaker and audience. They find it part of the process of taking to heart Dale Carnegie's rules for living.

Carnegie did everything he could to make his precepts easy to remember. Many of Carnegie's words sound like the wit and wisdom of Ben Franklin, even when they aren't. Echoes of parental wisdom fill the course. This advice never goes much deeper than "smile" or "give honest and sincere appreciation." Carnegie's familiar and comforting tone makes you feel you're embracing the tried and true.

Carnegie's lack of originality has kept him from appearing in the pages of *Bartlett's Familiar Quotations* (except by his title *How to Win Friends and Influence People*). In truth, as he readily admitted, he wasn't inventing principles. Some people have characterized the principles in *How to Win Friends* as derivative of the Golden Rule and those in *How to Stop Worrying* as restatements of "there's no use crying over spilt milk." Carnegie's achievement was not in formulating principles, but in devising an innovative group process that leads people to abide by his simple rules for living.

MEMORY SKILLS

Although it was a subject only tenuously connected to either public speaking or human relations, Carnegie also codified rules of memory. The goal was to provide people with simple rules to make it easy to remember names and concepts. The benefits would be increased confidence and freedom from dependence on notes.

What are memory skills doing in a course on effective speaking and human relations? Carnegie recognized that his course dealt more with self-confidence than any particular speaking or interpersonal skills. Consequently, he saw in what others have called "the lost arts of memory" a fruitful area to increase confidence quickly.

Teaching a specific skill in sessions one and two could generate tangible results immediately. It would involve class members more deeply in the course. To accomplish this skill building, he went back to a memory technique first taught by the Greeks.

The inventor of what's usually called the *loci* method of memorization was the poet named Simonides, or so Cicero reported. While attending a banquet, Simonides was called from the room. While he was outside the banquet hall, its roof collapsed, mangling the bodies inside beyond recognition. Simonides, however, was able to identify the bodies by remembering where each guest had sat.

This experience made Simonides aware of the power of visual memory. It gave him the idea that an individual could remember items by associating mental images of those items with particular places or loci. An orator, for example, could visualize objects that represented important points in a speech. He could place those objects in different rooms in a large building. To recall the points, you simply retraced your steps through the building. For most people, visual memory is stronger than verbal or physical memory and thus becomes an easy way to free oneself from notes.

What Carnegie brought into his course is an adaptation of the loci method called the peg system. In the peg system, you don't have to retrace your steps through a building to retrieve a particular item because you have placed items into a predetermined framework—pegging them to specific visual images.

Although the peg system has a distinguished history and impresses tens of thousands of Carnegie class members each year, the skills become rusty with disuse. Few graduates need to use memory skills every day, except in remembering names. Memory was a truly formidable power in the days when Cicero said, "Memory is the treasury and guardian of all things." Aeschylus was not exaggerating its importance when he said, "Memory is the mother of all wisdom." But today, it is relatively easy in contemporary America to get along with negligible formal memory skills.

REMEMBERING NAMES

The one memory skill still valued is remembering names. Many proponents of good business and human relations have emphasized it in the days since Dale Carnegie.

A New York University professor who published a book on *Improving the Memory for Faces and Names* several years before *How to Win Friends* appeared summed up the value of remembering names:

> It is hoped that this book will interest and help many people. Business and professional men whose dealings are directly with individuals obtain friendlier responses when they can name those with whom they speak. Executives secure better cooperation if they soften an order or put life into the impersonal tone of business by calling "Mr. Westfield" instead of shouting "Hey there." Social workers, teachers, and group leaders find their influence intensified through the personal feelings aroused by recalling the names of those about them. Young people just beginning to go about socially and starting that universal quest for popularity find a memory for names useful. It helps them to confidence and ease in meeting people.

The reasons today are the same. Who hasn't felt that awkwardness of greeting someone whose name you can't recall? Who hasn't felt less comfortable in a meeting or social situation because of not remembering the names of some participants? That discomfort has motivated many to work at the process of remembering names.

Unfortunately, it is a process, not an instant cure. When, in 1926, Carnegie first wrote about improving name-remembering abilities, he described the three natural laws of memory: impression, repetition, and association. He stated that every memory system has been based on these principles. Whether you take a seminar with one of the many memory experts selling their techniques, review *The Memory Book* by Harry Lorayne and Jerry

Lucas, or study one of the many other books on memory, you'll find that Carnegie was not far off the mark.

How do you learn name-remembering techniques? First, you decide that you *want* to remember a name. That will avoid the in-one-ear, out-the-other syndrome which usually means you never register the name. This resolution may mean asking someone to repeat his or her name when you're being introduced. It means concentrating on remembering someone's name as well as face. Since our visual memory is commonly stronger than our verbal memory, we usually have to put more energy into retaining the name than the face. Once we are sure we have the name and face, we move to what Carnegie, Lorayne, and others label association.

Hermine Hilton, an authority on memory and author of *The Executive Memory Guide*, calls this associative process of linking a name to something else we already know "categorization." She suggests the following headings as files into which we can mentally insert new names:

The same as someone I know?

The same as a celebrity?

An occupation (singer, shoemaker, smith)?

A thing (cane, woods, car)?

A brand name (Campbell, Kellogg, Ford)?

Can you rhyme it?

Can you convert it to a familiar word or words (Askew to ask you)?

Can you make a euphonious description (Jovial Jones, Smiling Smith)?

Can you translate it (Morgenstern is morning star)?

Does name-remembering work? Some class members finish the name-remembering session able to remember 90 percent or better of the names of thirty-five or more people they had never seen before that evening. And there are many success stories, such as the class member who carries off the task of introducing a group of twenty individuals he doesn't know well. Most people, however, save this skill for anxiety-provoking situations. Most of the time they don't use it.

The only problem with that strategy is that with memory as with any skill, if you don't use it, you'll lose it. And if you wait for the time when you really need it, you'll be rusty and not so likely to feel confident depending on it.

In contrast to their infrequent use of memory principles, most graduates continue to use the Dale Carnegie principles for controlling worry. Class members are quicker to see the rewards of controlling worry. The process of making a commitment to control worry in one's own life, followed by delivering a personal progress report and hearing of thirty-odd other progress reports, strongly reinforces the worry rules. The course treatment of worry enhances the ability of the group to facilitate change. With the rules of memory, the power of the group is not reinforced by a practical need. Thus the memory techniques, though intriguing, are often neglected after the student leaves the classroom.

CHAPTER 12

WHAT DO STEW LEONARD, LEE IACOCCA, AND CAROL COOK CARLISLE HAVE IN COMMON?

FROM THE MOMENT YOU DRIVE INTO THE 550-CAR parking lot in front of Stew Leonard's dairy store, you know you're about to visit a different kind of store. Large arrows show the traffic flow. An attendant directs you as if you're parking for a football game. When you step out of your car, the smells of baking bread and pastries greet you.

The first thing you see when you enter is a three-ton granite boulder. Carved into the rock is the store motto:

OUR POLICY

Rule 1
The Customer is Always Right

Rule 2
If the Customer Is Ever Wrong, Reread Rule 1

There is only one aisle in Stew Leonard's store. As you walk up the aisle, you can see, through windows, the in-house dairy where half-gallons of milk move along conveyer belts at 150 per minute. Above the frozen foods is an eight-foot-tall robot dog. It's playing the sort of county-fair music ("East Side, West Side") you'd hear at a Disneyland attraction. Stew Leonard's stocks only 700 or so items, compared to 10,000 to 15,000 for a normal grocery store. But when the store carries a product, it carries a lot of it. Stew Leonard tries to buy by the trailerload.

There are dozens of checkout stations. To keep his customers well served and happy, Leonard likes to keep at least twenty stations open all the time. As you check out, a clerk greets you with a wide smile. You have the feeling that your clerk genuinely wants you to have a good day as well as a good shopping experience.

Owner Stew Leonard generates outstanding performance from his employees. His management skills and philosophy have made him a celebrity, and his store's growth rate is a testament to his success. In twenty years, he has built a store with total sales of around $100 million. Sales per square foot hover at about ten times the industry average. He's now a management guru who has been quoted at length in business books and magazines. But a large part of his secret to success is a basic policy: he likes to have his employees take the Dale Carnegie Course.

During the course, his employees learn the sort of basics Dale Carnegie was teaching fifty years ago: Treat other people (that is, customers) the way you'd like them to treat you. It's the Golden Rule, via Carnegie, and Stew Leonard swears by it. "If I had never heard of Dale Carnegie, I would not have the business I have today."

Leonard was just twenty when he took the Dale Carnegie Course. The year he graduated from the University of Connecticut, his father died. Stew had to take over the family business, a home-delivery milk route. There were seven employees, most of them twice his age, and all resented that he was now their boss. His brother Leo suggested he read *How to Win Friends*. Then he took the course. "Today," Leonard says, "I wouldn't take a million dollars for what the course has taught me."

Over the years, Leonard has paid for hundreds of employees to take the course. Two walls at the store display their pictures.

Leonard believes in practicing the principles Carnegie espoused. An enthusiastic exponent of MBWA—management by wandering around—Leonard is continually working "to make employees happy, and make customers happy." Like Carnegie, Leonard relies on well-phrased aphorisms to get across his points. A favorite is: "If you chop enough wood for your neighbor, you end up with a nice big pile of wood chips for yourself."

Leonard also hires carefully. As he says, "We can teach cash register. We can't teach nice."

Leonard uses personnel evaluations to reinforce his approach. Everyone is measured on how they contribute to STEW: The S represents customer satisfaction; the T is for teamwork; the E is for excellence; and the W is for wow. Wow is to Stew Leonard what enthusiasm was to Dale Carnegie. It represents a sense of contagious excitement which can make the difference between success and mediocrity.

TRICKLE-DOWN
ENTHUSIASM

Dale Carnegie always relied on word of mouth to promote his course. The most effective promoters by far are those employers and executives like Stew Leonard who make the Dale Carnegie way part of the operating principles of their companies. Lee Iacocca, for example, induced dozens of employees and colleagues to take the course long before he praised it publicly in his autobiography.

This trickling down of enthusiasm for the course has made it almost a rite of passage to management levels in many companies. Yet when Iacocca signed up, it wasn't with the goal of learning the training methods in order to train other people.

Iacocca wanted it for himself. Like thousands of others through the years, he wanted, as he put it later, to stop being "an introvert, a shrinking violet."

Iacocca was in his early thirties. He had been assistant sales manager in Philadelphia for the Ford Motor Company and had received a promotion to national truck marketing manager in Detroit. Although his background was engineering, he now needed management skills to meet the challenge of his new job.

"I would rather teach engineers than anything," Carnegie once said, reflecting on his career. "I have taught 20,000 people personally . . . and always it was the engineers that I enjoyed teaching. That is because have you ever seen an insincere engineer? Besides, they're so bad to start with that it's a great joy to see them learn how to open their mouths without chewing their tongues up."

Lee Iacocca wasn't as ineffective as some of the engineers Carnegie mentioned. He had been on the debate team in high school. Yet Iacocca looked back on the course as a turning point. "The only way you can motivate people is to communicate with them" is how he put it. Becoming a better communicator made him a better manager.

AROUSE AN EAGER WANT

Stew Leonard, Lee Iacocca, and thousands of other business people leave the Dale Carnegie Course with a set of common-sense business principles. The principles reflect Carnegie's belief that to get results your employee or spouse or child must want to do what you have in mind. The authoritarian approach loses. The key is communicating or selling your ideas.

A fundamental theme in Dale Carnegie's books and courses is that each of us must use our powers and skill of persuasion to get things done. We have ideas to sell, spouses to persuade, bosses to convince, subordinates to motivate, children to direct. You don't have to be in sales to be in selling. You're doing it all the time.

The key to Carnegie's selling is arousing a want in the other person. Agreement to an order is not enough. According to the

Dale Carnegie philosophy, the other person has to *want* what you're selling.

From his class members and his research, Carnegie accumulated much anecdotal proof that his techniques worked. Carnegie developed a three-stage process to maximize those techniques. First, each class member makes a commitment in class to try a new approach. Second, each member shares his or her results. Third, each person listens to success stories from other class members.

A recent class member, Peter Young, reported on his ability to change the lackadaisical behavior of an administrative assistant. The assistant had been with the company twenty years and had a reputation as a heel-dragger.

Young told the class how he sparked a competitive spirit by challenging the assistant to help meet a team sales goal. "I had the feeling that Tom felt everyone had given up on him," Young said. "I told him that he could make the difference for us. I said if he would get the sales reports to the home office a day earlier, he would get us over the quota. We were that close. I also told him I'd buy him lunch if we made it. He did it, we did make it, and I treated him to a great lunch."

Cheryl Simons, another speaker in Young's class, was an account executive with a large advertising agency. One of her responsibilities was tracking the campaigns of two candy manufacturers who were competing with her client. Simons didn't have the time to do it, and her assistant, Frank, wasn't helping. Normally, Simons would have nagged Frank about his lack of cooperation. This time, she told the class, she had a change of heart:

> I was about to remind Frank about how he hadn't been keeping up with the project. Then I decided to apply some of what we'd been talking about in class. I decided to praise Frank for the organizational abilities he had demonstrated on another project. Then I mentioned to him how much our client valued the information he had been getting from us about our competitors. I told him how badly I felt that I wasn't able to keep up with it.

A week later, Frank gave me a three-ring binder, saying "Here it is." I was very happy. And the next time the client's product manager was in the office, I took a minute in front of Frank to tell the product manager that he had Frank to thank for the updated reports.

Summing up her progress report, Cheryl told the class: "My point is, begin with praise and honest appreciation, and you're more likely to accomplish what is important to you."

The reports of Peter and Cheryl were two of over thirty that evening. Like Cheryl ("begin with praise and honest appreciation"), each class member asks the class to do something. That message is reinforced by a benefit that accompanies the recommendation, showing there's a payoff for you ("you're more likely to accomplish what is important to you"). Each of these magic-formula talks follows Carnegie's technique for giving the audience an incentive to follow the recommended course of action. If you see the reward, you'll develop the want.

SELF-MOTIVATION

The Dale Carnegie Course teaches practical ways to motivate other people. But it also teaches self-motivation. The course helps people develop the self-confidence to tackle something new. It psychs them up to take a risk.

Carol Cook Carlisle took the course three years ago when she was unhappy in her job as special-events manager for a Fortune 500 company. She signed up for the course looking to improve her public-speaking skills. "A few weeks into the course," she reminisces, "I realized it wasn't the public speaking that I needed to focus on. It was the pressure."

For Carlisle, using Carnegie's principles to control worry helped deal with that pressure. As she dealt with the pressure, she discovered something she hadn't realized when she signed up for the course. She wanted to start her own special-events company. For her, the key was being able to think through the pressure.

"I thought about what might happen if the business failed. I decided the worst that could happen would be embarrassment. I could live with that. So against the advice of my husband and friends, I quit my job and started my business. I had no clients, but I felt I could make it work."

She did succeed. And she gives much credit to the course. "I wouldn't have opened the business—and it wouldn't still be open—without the course. It was the best thing I've ever done purely for myself."

For some people, the Carnegie books have been just as motivational as the course. John R. Johnson, chairman of the board of Chicago's Supreme Life Insurance Company, started a publishing business in 1942 with $500. Today, his publishing enterprise is one of the largest black-owned businesses in the United States. His publications include *Ebony* and *Jet*. Johnson used Carnegie to build his positive attitude. "In high school," says Johnson, "I read Dale Carnegie's *How to Win Friends and Influence People* at least fifty times."

POSITIVE THINKERS

Dale Carnegie promoted a philosophy of positive thinking founded on faith, trust, and the Golden Rule. His antecedents were religious thinkers rather than competitive, bottom-line-oriented businessmen. He was in the tradition of positive thinkers that includes Mary Baker Eddy, Norman Vincent Peale, and Robert Schuller.

Carnegie made a shrewd marketing decision. He avoided the religious labels that made positive thinking an exercise in belief. Carnegie didn't advocate mind cure or mind control. By presenting his ideas as homespun common sense, he maintained a broad appeal.

Nonetheless, much of his pedagogical approach depended on the techniques of mind cure that Mary Baker Eddy used in Christian Science. Mind cure grew up in the mid-nineteenth century when medicine was a far less effective science than it is today.

Essentially, mind cure is a faith—and the practices growing out of that faith—in the power of mind over body. Right thinking provides the power to heal yourself.

Dale Carnegie cared more about psychological than physical ills, but he applied the same power of the mind. He was forthright in acknowledging Mary Baker Eddy. He described her as "destined to have as much influence on the thinking of the world as any other woman who ever walked this earth."

He was quick to say that he was not proselytizing for Christian Science. At the same time, he proclaimed:

> But the longer I live, the more deeply I am convinced of the tremendous power of thought. As a result of thirty-five years spent in teaching adults, I know men and women can banish worry, fear, and various kinds of illnesses, and can transform their lives by changing their thoughts. I know! I know!! I know!!! I have seen such incredible transformations performed hundreds of times. I have seen them so often that I no longer wonder at them.

Carnegie clearly was a true believer. Asked once for the biggest lesson he had ever learned, he quoted the Roman philosopher Marcus Aurelius: "Our life is what our thoughts make it." And he cited Ralph Waldo Emerson: "A man is what he thinks about all day long." Like Mary Baker Eddy, Carnegie was not especially concerned with the reasons why faith or positive thinking could cure physical ailments or allow people to accomplish more. He approached the matter as a behaviorist. If he saw it work hundreds of times, well then, it worked.

POSITIVE THINKERS IN A SECULAR WORLD

Fortunately, Carnegie had several contemporaries who gave positive thinking an aura of professional expertise rather than religious fervor. During Carnegie's day, the notable proponents of positive thinking included a medical doctor, a psychotherapist, and a psychologist—Orison Marden, Emile Coué, and Henry Link.

Orison Marden, a graduate of Harvard Medical School, was a popular author and editor of *Success* magazine from 1897 to 1924. He built on the thoughts of various mind-cure writers in *Success* and in best-selling books such as *Pushing to the Front*. His message was clear: Never admit defeat; always feel powerful; think success. He felt that the will to succeed was the most vital single factor contributing to success.

Emile Coué was a French psychotherapist who had a sudden burst of popularity in the 1920s. He focused on the power of autosuggestion. He had millions of Americans repeating his mildly hypnotic phrase: "Day by day, in every way, I am getting better and better."

Carnegie risked being called another Coué when he encouraged people to repeat phrases such as "Act enthusiastic and you'll be enthusiastic." Carnegie was quick to reassure his readers that he wasn't trying to emulate Coué. But at the same time, if it worked, why not do it?

Carnegie's behavioral approach was very similar to that of another best-selling author, psychologist Henry Link. Link's *Return to Religion* appeared shortly before *How to Win Friends*. In 1937, when *How to Win Friends* was the best-selling nonfiction title of the year, *Return to Religion* was the third best-selling book.

Carnegie openly admired Link. He cited him extensively in both *How to Win Friends* and *How to Stop Worrying*. It's easy to see why Carnegie liked *Return to Religion*. It wasn't, as Carnegie assured his readers, some goody-goody book. It was simply a book of applied psychology. In truth, it had little to do with religion.

"A good personality," Link wrote, "is achieved by practice, not by introspection."

Link and Carnegie shared a bias for action. Link viewed modern psychology as moving "toward the emphasis on work, on doing things, as the road to happiness and away from the emphasis on thinking self-analysis, or talking oneself out of a difficulty." A positive thinker didn't have to worry about the causes of the problem, but could achieve success by focusing energy on the desired result—the solution to the problem—be it more money, more friends, or peace of mind.

THE PEALE APPROACH

Sixteen years after *How to Win Friends*, Norman Vincent Peale combined motivation and religion in a single, made-for-America package. *The Power of Positive Thinking*, written by the pastor of Marble Collegiate Church in Manhattan, surpassed the performance of *How to Win Friends* on the best-seller lists. Overnight, Reverend Peale became the inspirational guide to religious values for millions of Americans.

Carnegie and Peale knew each other, and, according to Peale, often commented to each other that they "were working both sides of the same street."

Carnegie and Peale had much in common. Both came from midwestern Christian homes where there was more religion than financial security. Separated from their roots, both clung to a preached tradition of strong values and firm conviction.

In each case, their books derived from their work with people. For Carnegie, the genesis was a course where thousands of adults came to him for public-speaking training and ended up with greater self-confidence and courage. For Peale, the roots were the thousands of individuals he had counseled as a minister at his church in Manhattan. He also learned from those who came to the religious-psychiatric clinic he had set up in the mid-1930s.

Both men tested their theories on people. They saw what helped people and what didn't. Then, through effective writing and speaking, they enthusiastically spread the word about what worked. Both were skilled in clearly conveying their messages to enormous numbers of people. Their simple language and memorable anecdotes convinced millions of people that these commonsense techniques could allow them to accomplish more of what was important to them.

Like Carnegie, Peale denied that he was teaching positive

thinking as a means to fame, riches, or power. The goals—materialistic or not—were up to the individual.

Peale believed a handful of principles could lead to a life full of joy and satisfaction, principles such as believe in yourself; stop fuming and fretting; expect the best and get it; relax for easy power. Like Carnegie, Peale's writing drew a cumulative power from dozens of everyday examples. Describing people who had used Peale's techniques, the minister described remarkable benefits possible with positive thinking.

The ideas of positive thinking that Peale and Carnegie spread so successfully are still strong in American culture. Peale is alive and active. He preaches and lectures, and his magazine *Guideposts* reaches over three million subscribers.

GOOD NEWS FROM SCHULLER

Author Robert Schuller is today's inheritor of the Carnegie-Peale tradition. Although he has changed the label to possibility thinking, the message is the same—*think positive*! The fundamentals of positive thinking are present in his best-selling books such as *Tough Times Never Last, But Tough People Do* and his popular television show "The Hour of Power." Like Carnegie, he reduces his precepts to aphorisms such as: "You won't win if you don't begin"; "The me I see . . . is the me I'll be"; and "When you've exhausted all possibilities, remember this, you haven't."

Recent programs such as Est and Silva Mind Control have taken some of the elements of positive thinking, mixed them with elements of encounter therapy and mysticism, and created major enterprises. Silva Mind Control, for example, claims to have over four million practitioners, with representation at major companies. José Silva, like Carnegie before him, uses Marcus Aurelius to try to convince us that our lives are what our thoughts make them. But he goes further than Carnegie. Where he, like Carnegie, declares, "Act enthusiastic and you'll be enthusiastic," he recommends simultaneously smiling and tapping your thymus for best results. Silva also adds a mystical component, as shown in this testimonial for applying mind control to interpersonal relations:

> I took a deep breath and as I exhaled I visualized a light around me. I saw it extending five or six feet around me. I programmed that everyone who came within that range would become more positive and more receptive to my working with them. It happened every time.

POSITIVE PEOPLE

In the Dale Carnegie Course, there is no such hocus pocus. All class members do, however, get a major dose of positive thinking in the course. In session six, for instance, each class member gives a report on how his or her attitude has become more positive in any area of life since the course began. Class members typically share experiences of handling a tough situation at work. Or they relate how positive thinking has given them the energy and motivation to play with the kids in the evening instead of watching television.

One class member, Frank Abernathy, summed up his reaction to the positive-thinking experiences in the following way: "You know, I'm a little bit surprised, but there really seems to be something to this positive thinking." Like many class members, he had never been immersed in an atmosphere of positive thinking. He had never read a self-help book or listened to a motivational cassette. But the Dale Carnegie approach eased him into accepting the approach, trying it out, and seeing it work.

Positive thinking has its critics, of course. A professor of leadership at Harvard Business School and also a psychoanalyst, Abraham Zaleznik says, "Positive thinking services as a valuable myth for people who believe it. But it may not necessarily lead people to deal with the realities of whatever they are good at."

Zaleznik criticizes some positive thinkers for not understanding that people must develop disciplines and talents. Some positive thinkers, he says, are "even holding out a false promise that it's easy: If I believe hard enough, I could become it. What non-sense!"

Carnegie never promised that positive thinking was an easy way out of learning skills. But he affirmed that skills were improved if people had a positive self-image and a strong positive drive. To an accountant in a recent course, Tony Franklin, the positive approach combined with his professional abilities to create exciting new opportunities for him.

Twelve weeks into the course, Franklin changed firms after ten years and bought his first house. The course didn't make Tony Franklin a better tax accountant or increase his financial resources. "It helped convince me," he said, "to make more of what I had going for me."

EPILOGUE: THE
AVERAGE MAN

TOWARD THE END OF HIS LIFE, DALE CARNEGIE WAS invited to speak at Marble Collegiate Church by its pastor, Dr. Norman Vincent Peale. For both men, it was an important occasion. Peale admired Carnegie's writing, and had been strongly influenced by his books and speeches. On his side, Carnegie regarded Peale as one of the leading spiritual leaders of the century. Carnegie was honored at being invited to preach.

The occasion had another significance for Carnegie. His mother had hoped that her son would become a minister. Although he had become famous for his public-speaking course and his books, Dale had never quite achieved his mother's dream.

Now, years after her death, her son was about to climb the pulpit of America's most famous minister.

It was one of the few occasions when Carnegie used notes. He carried six-by-eight-inch cards scrawled with his large, flowing script, one word per card. As he was later to tell Peale, "I wanted to be sure of myself that day."

Although Carnegie had planned thoroughly, emotion overwhelmed him in the middle of his sermon. He began talking about his childhood in Missouri. He recalled times when his family scarcely had food enough to put on the table. He told the congregation how his mother sang hymns as she went about her work. He repeated her belief that "the Lord would provide."

At that point, Peale recalls:

> Dale had to stop. A dead silence prevailed. He was overcome by emotion. The circumstance of being in church and speaking about his mother from that pulpit—the whole setting—conspired to move him deeply.
>
> Struggling with tears, he finally said, "My parents gave me no money nor financial inheritance, but they gave me something of much great value, the blessing of faith and sturdy character."
>
> This had a tremendous effect on the congregation. The sentiment was unforgettable. It was one of the most moving and affecting speeches I have ever heard.

In some important ways, this sermon was the culmination of Carnegie's career. While he had not become a minister or missionary, in a roundabout way he at last fulfilled his mother's ambitions. The poor farmboy from Missouri had finally made it.

Yet this moment also had all the usual Carnegie contradictions. The teacher who had made a lifelong habit of speaking spontaneously used note cards for the one great sermon of his life. America's most noted public speaker became speechless. Although he had given thousands of people the confidence to stand up and speak before audiences, words failed him at this critical moment.

Who was Dale Carnegie—inspiring preacher or incurable sentimentalist? Leader or follower? Success or failure? Perceptive teacher or perpetual student?

The best answer is that Dale Carnegie, by almost all measures, was an average man. Throughout his life, he could speak powerfully and movingly, but he could not find words for the emotions that moved him most strongly. Fame pulled him up, but natural humility dragged him down. Thirst for education pushed him forward, but the need to belong pulled him back. His restless energy made him ambitious, but his generous good nature put the lid on aggressiveness.

None of these conflicts could stifle his growth as a teacher or slow the momentum of his ambitions in business. The net result was an individual who sheltered—rather than expressed—his warring impulses. Yet there was still something that made him different from other average men. Rather than keeping these impulses entirely to himself, he presented them to the world in the form of a course.

Taken piece by piece, session by session, exercise by exercise, the Dale Carnegie Course is more than the creative expression of Dale Carnegie. It is also the end product of his warring impulses. The course takes students to various extremes. In one session, they are urged to express rage and frustration; in another, to give others their full cooperation. One exercise glorifies ham acting; another, sincere personal confession. At one extreme, the Dale Carnegie Course teaches persuasive tactics for winning compliance. At the other, it preaches the virtues of being empathic.

Although the Dale Carnegie Course takes people to such extremes, it also brings them back again. Having stretched and challenged people, it reminds them of their own worth and reinforces their personal goals. Each person comes with his or her own expectations and graduates with different resolutions. Some leave the course searching for greater security, others for greater risk. Some seek leadership skills, while others seek new leaders to follow. There are those who want more success, prosperity, and recognition; others set their sights on being more honest, generous, or forgiving.

The certificate that students receive upon completion does

not certify competence or expertise in any particular area. It is simply a recognition that the student has stuck with the course to the end. Far from changing significantly, many students finish the course just feeling happier or more content to be themselves.

For Dale Carnegie, creating the course helped resolve many conflicts in his own life. In his classrooms, he could be preacher, missionary, teacher, confidant, actor, business leader, psychologist, philosopher, and writer. The very qualities that made him average helped him create a course with universal appeal. It took an average man to understand what would ultimately influence millions, and it took an average man to communicate with a mass audience. Although he would never be an outstanding orator, a brilliant writer, a notable politician, or a man of letters, the course helped him accept himself for who he was.

Today, more than a hundred years since Dale Carnegie was born, his course is still helping millions of individuals do the same.

INDEX